Energy
Security

Energy Security

—— Roland Dannreuther ——

polity

First published in 2017 by Polity Press

Polity Press
65 Bridge Street
Cambridge CB2 1UR, UK

Polity Press
350 Main Street
Malden, MA 02148, USA

ISBN-13: 978-0-7456-6190-2(pb)
ISBN-13: 978-0-7456-6191-9

A catalogue record for this book is available from the British Library.

Typeset in 11 on 13 pt Sabon
by Toppan Best-set Premedia Limited
Printed and bound in Great Britain by Clays Ltd, St Ives PLC.

The publisher has used its best endeavours to ensure that the URLs for external websites referred to in this book are correct and active at the time of going to press. However, the publisher has no responsibility for the websites and can make no guarantee that a site will remain live or that the content is or will remain appropriate.

Every effort has been made to trace all copyright holders, but if any have been inadvertently overlooked the publisher will be pleased to include any necessary credits in any subsequent reprint or edition.

For further information on Polity, visit our website:
politybooks.com

Contents

Figures and Tables

Figures

Tables

Acknowledgements

My interest in energy politics emerged relatively late in my career and is primarily due to Philip Andrews-Speed, and I am grateful for his support and for our productive intellectual collaboration. This included the EU-funded *Polinares* project (2010–13) where I also met a number of energy specialists who have had a considerable influence on the evolution of my thought. I would like to express my particular gratitude in this regard to Paul Stevens, David Humphreys, Giacomo Luciani, Evelyne Dietsche and Patrick Criqui. A special mention is to be given to Wojciech Ostrowski who has been a colleague, friend and support throughout the gestation of this book and encouraged me when my spirits were lagging.

– 1 –
Introduction

Energy security is a value that is highly prized by states, societies and individuals. Our modern civilization is critically dependent on the energy resources and the energy services that make our lives prosperous and worthwhile. The systems and networks that have developed to ensure this flow of modern energy have become increasingly more complex and transnational. Oil and gas pipelines cross national borders; very large tanker ships transport oil, gas and coal over the world's oceans; and electricity grids criss-cross nations and continents. These resources and networks also represent large and profitable business opportunities, with companies and states competing to protect and expand their market share. And these energy flows, the majority of which are based on fossil fuels, interact with our environment in increasingly serious and unpredictable ways.

All of this creates vulnerabilities and anxieties that make energy security such a critical concern. This has also been evident since the end of the Cold War and the beginning of the new millennium. The sources of this heightened sense of vulnerability and anxiety are multiple. They include the volatility of the price of key energy resources, with the price of a barrel of oil rising from below $20 in the late 1990s to a peak of $148 in 2008 and then dropping to below $30 in 2014. This price volatility has paralleled severe political instability in many of the most significant energy-producing regions of the world. The petroleum-rich Middle East has been in almost ceaseless turmoil since the turn of the new century with multiple wars, revolutions and the spread of virulent forms of terrorism. A number of other key strategic energy-rich countries have become increasingly in conflict with the West, such as Russia in the aftermath of its intervention into Ukraine in 2014.

All of this is complicated by the changes in the profile of the major global energy consumers. While in the past these were primarily Western countries, the 2000s saw the rise of the emerging Asian economies as the most dynamic source for increased energy demand. The economic transformation of China has been the most dramatic illustration of this, leading to a radical re-directing of global energy flows to the Chinese mainland. The energy security dimensions of this are a new element in global international energy politics.

Energy security anxieties also extend to longer-term and more existential concerns. The growth of the global economy in the 1990s and 2000s, leading to the rising cost of energy commodities, resurrected fears of impending scarcity and the belief that a 'peak' in the production of these key resources is being reached. This presentiment of impending scarcity has been exacerbated by the scientific evidence that our continuing dependence on fossil fuels is irreparably damaging the natural environment through the greenhouse gas emissions that contribute to global warming. This sense of impending crisis is in turn often linked to a concern that the technical complexity of our energy systems is making us more vulnerable. For example, the Fukushima nuclear accident in 2011 confirmed a widespread suspicion over the safety and reliability of dependence on nuclear sources of energy. There is also a wider recognition that our modern energy systems embed deeply unequal and unjust social, economic and political relations. While the advanced developed world enjoys a superfluity of energy services, there are over 1.4 billion of the poorest who lack basic access to electricity and over 2.4 billion who do not benefit from modern cooking services. For these poorest of our global population, energy security is not an exceptional occurrence but a daily existential challenge.

Aim and Structure of the Book

Energy Security is a book that differs from much of the expansive academic literature on energy security in that it is single-authored and does not incorporate a collection of differing perspectives from a variety of authors. There are an increasing number of high-quality multi-authored handbooks or collections on energy security or associated energy-related themes (Goldthau and Witte 2009b; Sovacool 2011; Goldthau 2013; Ekins et al. 2015; Kuzemko et al. 2016; Van de Graaf et al. 2016). The advantage of these multi-authored collections is that they are comprehensive in their range and scope, dealing with the multiple perspectives and dimensions that are integral to the complex interdependencies of energy studies. However, they can often lack a clear overarching narrative or argument as the different authors reflect their particular and distinctive views and perspectives (for an exception, see Bradshaw 2014).

The driving purpose of this book is to articulate an overarching conception and narrative of energy security. It is a conception which highlights in particular the political and contested nature of energy security. The central themes are those of power and justice and how considerations of the distribution of power and the perceptions of justice or injustice are critical for understanding or seeking to address issues of energy security. It is a perspective that, with the priority accorded to politics, draws in particular from the disciplines of International Relations and security studies while recognizing that any comprehensive understanding of energy security needs to draw from multiple disciplines. It is an approach which also accords a particular weight to history and how our understandings of energy security, with the associated power and justice concerns, are rooted in and suffused with historical legacies and developments. The book also focuses on how to combine the material physicality of the energy resources that underpin energy security and the social, economic and political environment in which understandings and narratives of energy security are constructed.

In pursuing this overarching argument and narrative, the scope of the book does nevertheless cover an ambitious range of different aspects and dimensions of energy security. However, with the main aim of the book being to focus on a political dimension which is at times absent from other accounts, this does mean that not all the different aspects of energy security are always covered with equal weight. For example, some of the more technical aspects of energy security have not been given focused attention, such as the role of international regimes in providing for oil storage or how grid management systems can manage intermittent renewable power sources. In addition, though issues of energy access to the poorest peoples are highlighted as a central concern that impacts on energy security, this issue is not analysed in depth. However, these gaps are compensated by the book's focus on the often neglected political dimensions of energy security and the new perspectives that this approach provides.

In developing this overarching argument and analysis, chapter 2 is particularly important in introducing the analytical framework and theoretical underpinnings of the book. As noted above, the framework is drawn mainly from the discipline of International Relations and from theoretical scholarship in international security studies. The advantages of the security studies approach is that it extends the scope of security beyond the traditional Cold War preoccupation with military conflict to new forms of security. It also recognizes that security is not an objective but a socially constructed reality and that our conceptualizations of security are framed and influenced by our social, economic and political conditions. *Energy Security* is a book whose central preoccupation is with the politics of energy security. However, this focus is not exclusive and insights are drawn from different disciplinary perspectives – such as economics, law, geography and sociology – recognizing the fact that energy security cannot be addressed without taking an interdisciplinary approach.

A distinctive feature of *Energy Security* is that it brings to the foreground the contested and normative nature of energy security. It takes seriously the view that energy security is an inextricably political concern involving questions of 'who gets what, when, and how'. The underlying assumption is that energy security involves differing and unequal relations of political power, divergent understandings of justice and fairness, and conflicts over differing values. Chapter 2 gives analytical expression to this through the application of the main theoretical traditions of International Relations to energy security. These theoretical perspectives, it is argued, provide differing prisms through which to understand energy security and incorporate within them the main tensions and conflicts over energy security. The recognition of differing perspectives and narratives of energy security also dissolves the idea that there is a single correct conceptualization of energy security. As such, the chapter concludes by arguing that energy security needs to be understood as one value competing with other core values, such as economic prosperity and sustainability. A distinctive feature of this book is the prominence it gives to considerations of power and justice in its analytical framework.

Chapter 3 draws this out by assessing the evolution of energy security in its broader historical context. A strong theme of *Energy Security* is the importance accorded to history and how the legacies of the past continue to influence the ways in which energy security is currently conceptualized and debated. The chapter illustrates how differing historically defined energy systems, dependent on particular dominant energy resources, construct differing forms of energy insecurity. The chapter starts by thinking about energy security in the pre-modern and pre-industrial age and the transformation that occurred with the industrial coal-driven age. The energy security concerns over dependence on coal radically changed with the next major transition to the oil age and the growing international security concerns as regards the concentration of oil reserves in the Middle East. This culminates in the first major energy security crisis in the 1970s when there was a major shift in geo-economic power from the energy-importing Western countries to the energy-producing countries, in particular to those countries grouped within the Organization of the Petroleum Exporting Countries (OPEC). The chapter concludes by explaining how this crisis was overcome and the West reasserted its dominance through a mix of economic diversification and political and ideological developments.

The next two chapters are dedicated to an analysis of the more immediate political dimensions of contemporary energy insecurity, with chapter 4 examining energy security in terms of international security and contemporary inter-state relations, and chapter 5 in terms of domestic security and relations between states and their societies. Chapter 4 identifies the ways in which energy security has affected, and has been affected by, three major contemporary sources of international insecurity. The first is the instability and conflict in the Middle East; the second, China's rise as a major power and its expansion as a global energy player; and the third, Russia's increasing use of energy as a source of geopolitical power and the deterioration in its relations with the West. Chapter 5 shifts attention from inter-state to intra-state domestic politics and argues how energy security also has a domestic political dimension. This is because energy resources are valuable commodities and thus inevitably foster internal social,

economic and political conflicts over the equitable distribution and use of these resources. This chapter engages in
particular with the debates over the so-called 'resource
curse' and the argument that resources are not only increasingly becoming a source of domestic conflict but also a
cause of civil wars.

Chapters 6 and 7 direct attention from the social and
political to the economic and environmental dimensions
of energy security. Chapter 6 examines the complex ways
in which energy security concerns interact with relations
between states and energy markets. This chapter is more
granular than other chapters in that it assesses this through
an analysis of the major energy resources; coal, oil, nuclear,
gas and renewables. This chapter connects in particular
with chapter 3 as it takes a quasi-historical approach,
focusing on oil and coal first, and then looking at the more
recently developed energy sources of natural gas, nuclear
and modern renewables. Indeed, some readers might wish
to read this chapter immediately after the historical chapter,
particularly for those wanting to gain a better understanding of the specificities of these differing energy resources
and flows. The main conclusion of this chapter is that
states have generally sought to promote energy security
through expanding and diversifying their energy mix rather
than displacing any of these resources. Energy security
cannot also be divorced from considerations of economic
competitiveness and the critical role of energy markets.

Chapter 7 assesses whether this incremental and cautious approach to energy security is ultimately environmentally sustainable. This involves engaging with two
major debates; the first on whether there are limits to the
supply of the fossil fuels that underpin our contemporary
energy-intensive modern industrial systems; the second on
how to avert damaging anthropogenic climate change
through the reduction and, ultimately, the elimination of
the carbon dioxide emissions generated by fossil fuels.
While the notion that we have reached a geological 'peak'
and are 'running out' of fossil fuels is not supported in this

chapter, it does nevertheless argue that there needs to be some 'peak fossil fuels', not least so as to stem global warming. The chapter then assesses the substantial efforts to negotiate an international agreement on climate change, most notably through the Kyoto Protocol, and why the actual impact on global emissions has been so limited. The chapter concludes by noting that, though there are reasons to be pessimistic that sufficient measures will be put in place to avert climate change, there are nevertheless some sources of optimism as well.

Overall, *Energy Security* seeks to articulate this larger landscape of energy security, locating it within a global, regional and national political framework. Energy security is understood as a value that is in continual competition with other values, such as economic prosperity and sustainability, and where the legacies of history, power inequalities and concerns over distributive justice play crucial roles in framing what we understand by the concept. In the final analysis, it is the intellectual excitement of grappling with energy security and its multiple dimensions that this book seeks, however imperfectly, to convey.

– 2 –

Energy Security: An Analytical and Theoretical Framework

One of the immediate problems with energy security is defining the meaning and the scope of the concept. It is a frequently stated truism that energy security is a multi-dimensional phenomenon (Baumann 2008; Chester 2010). The challenge is to identify and then classify or categorize these different dimensions. A leading handbook on energy security illustrates the extent of the challenge as it identifies the following nine dimensions: climate change, sustainable development, maritime, public policy, diversification, environmental, energy poverty, social development, energy services and industrial (Sovacool 2011). This reflects, as the editor notes, the different ways of approaching energy security and whether one adopts a scientific, economic, ecological, social welfare or geopolitical perspective (see also Sovacool 2016). Energy security can also be seen to have a temporal dimension, with differing analyses as to whether the perceived risks or threats are short-term or long-term in nature. There is also a question of scale and whether energy security is being examined at a global level or at a local level or at a level somewhere in-between. Even at the basic level of a clear definition of energy security, there are a multiplicity of competing definitions and no universally accepted core definition.

One common attempt to bring some degree of order to the complex multi-dimensional nature of energy security is to isolate four key elements within the concept. There is some variation in the descriptors for these four elements with, for example, Jonathan Elkind promoting a widely used categorization of availability, reliability, affordability and sustainability (Elkind 2010), while others have adopted similar terms such as availability, accessibility, affordability and acceptability (Bridge and Le Billon 2013: 93–124). What these usefully do is to bring together some of the principal dimensions of energy security into a simpler taxonomy, which separates the geopolitical from the more systems-specific and environmental and energy poverty dimensions of energy security. However, despite the clear utility of these categorizations, they remain essentially technical exercises in taxonomy and do not provide a theoretical grounding of the concept of energy security. From the perspective of this book, they do not sufficiently anchor energy security in its broader political setting and do not bring to the foreground the interaction of energy security, power and justice, which is the central theme of the book.

This chapter seeks to develop this more theoretically grounded analysis through locating energy security in the theoretical literature within security studies and more generally within the discipline of International Relations. The chapter starts with a recognition that the concept is, indeed, multi-dimensional and argues that three distinctions in the application of the concept need critically to be incorporated: the political and discrete as against the systemic and general applications of energy security; energy security as applied to different energy sources; and the distinction between the security of the supply of energy resources and the supply of energy services. The second section reflects on the increasingly complex and multi-faceted meanings of energy security and argues that this dynamic is mirrored in the shift in security studies from a traditional military or geopolitical conception of security to non-traditional and broader conceptions of security. This is then followed by how these differing conceptions of security, including energy security, are driven by differing normative theoretical conceptions or perspectives of security which can be mapped onto the International Relations theoretical frames of realism, liberalism and radicalism. The chapter concludes by arguing that energy security needs to be understood as a value and a value which competes with other values. As such, energy security competes and is in continual tension with the values of prosperity or economic efficiency, with the value of sustainability, and with the value of justice. It is, in particular, how justice and the realities of power interact with energy security which are often neglected but essential for understanding energy security.

Defining Energy Security

There is no single, comprehensive definition of energy security that does justice to its multi-dimensional and complex nature. The more productive way to approach this definitional problem is to distinguish clearly between the differing ways in which the concept is applied in practice. Three distinctions are particularly relevant in this regard.

The Political and the Systemic

The first is to recognize that the meaning and definition of energy security differs significantly whether applied to the perceived risks and threats that come from deliberate, intentional acts as against those that are more indirect, unintentional and complex. In practice, this is less of a binary distinction and more of a continuum from one extreme to the other. The best way to try and explain this is through concrete examples. At one end of the spectrum, energy security focuses on threats from an intentional

political decision of an actor, normally a state, to undermine the supply of energy which would clearly harm the
energy interests of other states (Cherp and Jewell 2011:
1–3). A high-profile example of this would be the threat
that Iran could decide to take military action to cut off the
Strait of Hormuz, the vital sea channel between the Persian
Gulf and the Indian Ocean, which would severely disrupt
the export of oil from the Persian Gulf and thereby create
a major energy security crisis for oil-consuming states. For
the United States, the gravity of this threat is taken so seriously that it is clearly understood as a *casus belli*, justifying
an immediate military response. Another highly topical
and frequently discussed example is the threat, already
partially enacted in 2007 and 2009, that Russia could
take a political decision to cut off gas supplies to Ukraine
which would represent a major threat to European energy
interests.

It is important to note that the threat of deliberate
intentional political acts undermining energy security is
not limited to large energy-producing states with anti-
Western agendas. The Chinese leadership, for example,
takes seriously and believes that there are credible circumstances in which the United States could decide to impose
a military embargo on the Malacca Straits in the context
of a larger political and military crisis between Washington
and Beijing (Lanteigne 2008: 144). Threats to energy security can also impact on energy-producing as well as energy-
consuming states, affecting and harming their energy
security interests. For example, the political decisions to
apply sanctions, such as on the energy sectors of Iran or
Russia, damages the energy security interests of producing
states. These energy security interests are rather differently
articulated from the large energy-consuming states as the
concern is principally for 'security of demand' rather than
'security of supply'. For these countries, a longer-term
energy security threat is the European Union's political
ambition to reduce its dependence on fossil fuels and to
engage in so-called 'demand destruction' so as to meet its

ambitious carbon emissions reduction targets. If success-fully implemented, this would undoubtedly represent a threat to the interests of the traditional energy suppliers to European markets, such as the Gulf states and Russia.

This last example actually represents a move along the continuum from the intentional and political to the unin-tentional and systemic. This other end of the spectrum incorporates those risks and threats that are not driven by intentional and discrete state-driven political acts but are the consequences of complex interactions of multiple systems, actors and processes. The way that climate change intersects with energy security is an example of the extreme of this continuum. The issue here is how the unintentional consequences of the totality of the systems underpinning the development of modern industrial civilization, based critically as it has been on the utilization of the power of the energy embedded in fossil fuels, has gradually but inexorably contributed to the warming of the planet's climate. This is generally recognized as a serious existential threat to all humanity. The notion that we have entered into an 'Anthropocene age' articulates the unprecedented complexity of these systemic challenges as it articulates how human-influenced systems, including the human-constructed energy systems, are for the first time directly affecting the earth's ecosystems (Steffen et al. 2007; Zala-ziewicz et al. 2011). The concept of the Anthropocene highlights that a clear distinction between human and natural ecological systems is no longer valid and that our energy systems in particular affect both. Energy security that incorporates this global and ecological systemic aspect clearly is very different in its scope and meaning from when applied in its more immediate political context.

Even without the added complexity of climate change, modern energy systems are themselves very complicated and interconnected, particularly when understood in terms of the entirety of the energy supply chain and its infra-structure. For example, the energy systems of the United States include, as Daniel Yergin points out, 'more than

150 refineries, 4,000 offshore platforms, 160,000 miles of oil pipelines, facilities to handle 15 million barrels of oil a day of imports and exports, 10,400 power plants, 160,000 miles of high-voltage electric power transmission lines and millions of miles of electric power distribution wires, 410 underground gas storage fields, and 1.4 million miles of natural gas pipelines' (Yergin 2006: 78). Figure 2.1 illustrates just one dimension of this: the gas pipeline network in the US. Ensuring the security of such a complicated and integrated system is itself an inherently complex operation, involving highly technical specialist knowledge, a sophisticated and voluminous set of legal and regulatory frameworks, and the cooperation and coordination of a multiplicity of actors. Despite all precautionary measures, the unexpected and unpredictable inevitably at times challenge the security and integrity of such complex systems, such as the effects of hurricanes or the tsunami which overwhelmed the Fukushima nuclear power plant in Japan in 2011 (Tanter 2013). Electricity black-outs can also occur unexpectedly as a consequence of poor policy decisions, such as in California in 2001 when many parts of the

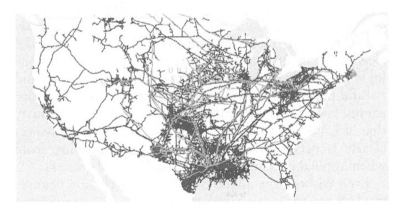

Figure 2.1 US Natural Gas Pipelines
Source: Energy Information Administration, Office of Oil and Gas, National Gas Division, Gas Transportation Information System

state suffered shortages as a consequence of the flaws in the design and implementation of the deregulation of the electricity market in that state (Nye 2010).

Energy security does, therefore, need to be differently understood as it has distinct meanings depending on whether it is applied to risks or threats that are political and discrete as against the systemic and complex. At the discrete and intentional end of the spectrum, the nature of the energy security challenges tends to be more immediate, more clearly identifiable and intellectually graspable; at the other end of the spectrum, the challenges are more difficult to assess, more complex and multi-layered, and require more complex policy responses. Nevertheless, what is constant across the spectrum is that the challenges remain ultimately political in nature, though the politics might involve the application of differing instruments, from the military at one end to the legal and regulatory at the other.

Different Energy Sources

A second important distinction to be made involves the recognition that when speaking about energy security the principal referent is normally to specific sources of energy. There are, though, significant differences in how the concept of energy security is applied relative to the particular energy source being considered. There is, first, the particularity of the energy source itself, whether it be oil, gas, coal, nuclear or the different forms of renewable energy. There is, second, the ways in which energy security is applied in different ways according to the particular activities along the global value chain. These typically extend from exploration to production, transportation, processing and consumption. A third element is the actual value of the source whether defined in terms of its market price or in terms of economic rent.

Of all the major energy sources, it is oil which has undoubtedly pride of place in terms of concerns over energy security. A significant factor behind this is the economic value of oil which dwarfs those of other energy sources. Almost seven out of every ten barrels of oil is exported, representing the largest component of international trade. Oil is also associated, both at popular and elite level, with wealth and global and social inequality. This is captured by the concept of rent which, as an economic term, means the payment to a factor of production in excess of the cost needed to bring that factor into production. Oil provides a classic example of high economic rent. In Saudi Arabia, the actual cost of production for a barrel of oil is close to $10 a barrel but the price paid for that on international markets is vastly greater (at its height in 2008 at $147). Naturally such profits and 'unearned' wealth derived from oil in Saudi Arabia and other Gulf states generates resentment and envy from other less resource-rich states. The fact that the main reserves of oil are geographically located in some of the most politically unstable parts of the world adds to the association of oil with energy insecurity. For many, the abiding image of energy security is through the association of oil and the Middle East. These anxieties are further compounded by the common belief that oil is a scarce and diminishing resource and that the world might have already passed 'peak' production (see chapter 7; and also Campbell and Laherrere 1998; Bridge 2010).

Energy security concerns over oil are also found at the demand end of the value chain. This is because there is limited demand elasticity due to the fact that the transportation sector, meaning essentially cars, lorries and planes, overwhelmingly relies on oil. There has so far been limited success in developing alternatives in this sector. However, it is important to note that not all parts of the value chain for oil generate serious energy security concerns. As many commentators note, the oil market, once oil reaches the world's oceans, is one of the most global and efficient (Goldthau and Witte 2009a: 375–6). Oil is freely and efficiently transported from one part of the world to the other and it is very difficult to intervene politically or militarily to disrupt that flow. The attempts to use oil as a 'weapon' have generally always failed because of the strength and fungibility of the market (Al-Sowayegh 1984; Smith Stegen 2011).

This is, though, in contrast to gas where it is precisely in this area of the international transportation of gas supplies that the most serious energy security concerns are to be found. This can be illustrated in relation to Russian energy supplies to Europe. In reality, Russian oil exports to Europe generate far greater revenues and are economically much more significant for the Russian state than gas exports. However, European consuming states are generally not very anxious about the potential for the politically motivated disruption of oil supplies from Russia as oil shortfalls could relatively easily be compensated through supplies from other producing regions. But there is much greater anxiety about the potential threat of a gas cut-off as Russian gas is supplied through fixed intercontinental pipelines and involves long-term contractual arrangements (Newnham 2011; Schmidt-Felzmann 2011). For those European countries particularly dependent on Russian gas supplies, securing alternative supplies is both expensive and would require significant time and investments. The failure of the EU to secure the funding and support for the development of an alternative Nabucco gas pipeline from the Middle East and the Caucasus illustrates well the difficulties of diversifying away from Russia (Dickel et al. 2014).

Other energy sources have their own similarly distinctive energy security challenges and dimensions. For nuclear energy, the most serious risks come not from the production or transportation of the fuel but at the processing stage when there is a danger that countries might seek to produce highly enriched weapons grade uranium and thus undermine the nuclear international proliferation norm as institutionalized in the Nuclear Non-Proliferation Treaty. There are also serious risks over the safety of nuclear generating plants, particularly after the accidents at Chernobyl in 1986 and Fukushima in 2011. How safely to store and protect future generations from the radiation dangers of spent nuclear fuel is also a very difficult practical longer-term security question. Modern renewables do not have such long-term legacies but, in particular with wind and solar, the prevalent energy security concern is over the intermittency and variability of the supply of wind and sun, which means that alternative and potentially expensive back-ups need to be factored in.

Coal again provides its own distinctive energy security concerns. In practice, coal is relatively rarely incorporated into energy security calculations as coal is relatively inexpensive, abundant and geographically much more widely distributed across different countries than oil or gas. Only 15 per cent of coal is traded internationally as against 60 per cent of oil. Indeed, many developing countries, such as India and China, rely heavily on their domestic coal resources for electricity generation and the availability of this local resource is viewed as a vital element in their energy security. However, where coal does become a serious energy security concern is in its contribution to environmental degradation and to the global growth in carbon emissions, as coal is the dirtiest of the fossil fuels. Indeed, coal represents one of the most significant tensions between energy security, as conceptualized from a national perspective, and energy security conceptualized at a global systemic level incorporating the threat posed by climate change. Energy security has to incorporate this global environmental dimension and this is where coal's role in both supporting and adversely affecting energy security is a particularly acute political issue.

Energy Sources and Energy Services

The third distinction to be made is between energy security as applied to energy fuels, such as oil and gas, and as applied to the services that these energy sources support. In a sense, this could reasonably be argued to be a more legitimate focus for concerns over energy security as energy resources are not inherently valuable in themselves but are valuable for the services and benefits that they offer. These services include most of the advances in prosperity and well-being of our modern industrial civilization – services such as heating, transportation, communications, food, consumer products and housing. In a modern society, the enormous increases to the collective social well-being that these services provide are ultimately underpinned by, and would not be possible without, the modern energy systems on which they depend. If the problem of energy security is defined in this way, in terms of ensuring the minimization of risk to these energy-dependent services, then it is not the rich industrialized world that truly suffers from energy insecurity. In practice, it is rare that prosperous citizens in the North suffer anything more than intermittent interruptions to such services.

This is not the case in many parts of the poorer developing world. It is estimated that 1.4 billion people lack access to electricity and 2.4 billion do not enjoy modern cooking services (Bhattacharyya 2013: 228). For these people, the lack of such services, in part due to the lack of access to modern energy systems like the electricity grid, is a very serious source of individual insecurity. This includes the insecurity of having to search for reliable supplies of energy; the health implications of the need to collect and use wood or other biomass sources; and the poverty and lack of opportunity that come from being disconnected from the networks for social advancement. It is here that energy insecurity has a strongly developmental dimension and where energy poverty converges to a significant degree with the concept of energy security (Pachauri 2010).

Energy Security and Debates in Security Studies

As these various differing dimensions of energy security demonstrate, the concept is fluid and diverse, ranging from energy poverty, to broader systemic issues such as climate change, and to specific geopolitical and military-related concerns. If the emergence of these differing dimensions is plotted over time, the concept has itself a historical trajectory of increasing complexity and of a more multi-faceted scope. Energy security first gained a general popular resonance during the 1970s with the rise of OPEC, the rapid increase in oil prices, and conflict and war in the Middle East. In this context, energy security had a clear political focus linked to oil and shifts in geopolitical power. Since the 1970s, the environmental movement has grown in prominence and the issue of the contribution of fossil fuels to environmental degradation has become a more prominent issue, prompting shifts in the scope of the meaning of energy security. Nuclear disasters such as at Chernobyl in 1986 brought in the more systemic risks of the complexity of modern energy systems. Post-Cold War civil wars in Sub-Saharan Africa and elsewhere engendered greater attention to the linkages between security and development and, in relation to energy, the links between energy poverty and energy insecurity.

Such widening and expansion of the concept of energy security reflects broader developments in the field of security studies. During the Cold War, security was primarily viewed through the prism of military threats to security. The key focus was on the prospect of military confrontation with the Soviet Union and it was natural that the threat of nuclear conflagration and a possible World War III dominated security studies. This focus on a European-centred threat of war did change with the onset of wars of liberation in the colonial world and the increased level of confrontation between North and South, including the challenge presented by OPEC. Nevertheless, security was still primarily understood in military terms and within the broader context of the bipolar Cold War confrontation.

With the end of the Cold War, this dominant focus on military security began to change and there was a counter-movement which argued that security should no longer be limited to the military domain and that there were more urgent non-military and non-traditional security risks and threats which needed to be addressed. The global threat of environmental degradation, particularly in relation to climate change but also including concerns such as over-population and water scarcity, represented the first significant non-traditional and non-military expansion of security studies (Mathews 1989; Homer-Dixon 2001). During the 1990s, the growing fears of mass migration led to demands that this deep anxiety and insecurity over national identities needed also to be incorporated into the study of security (Huysmans 2000). In addition, the problems and insecurities of those suffering from civil wars and deprivation in Sub-Saharan Africa and elsewhere led to demands that security needed to have a stronger focus on their needs and demands. This became part of a broader critique of traditional security studies as excessively privileging the security interests of states when it is often states that are the principal sources of insecurity. Instead of state security, the demand was for security studies to focus on 'human security' and to take as the primary reference the insecurities of individuals as they struggle with conflict and under-development (Commission on Human Security 2003).

Security studies has, therefore, generally broadened and widened in similar ways to the changes in the meanings of energy security. Some have argued that this has been a negative development, making the study of security incoherent and increasing the danger that military responses might be considered for problems which require very different tools and instruments (Levy 1995). Although there is a certain legitimacy to such concerns, there is a practical limit to the degree to which it is possible to go back to more limited and traditional conceptions of security. Indeed, one of the most important insights that this post-Cold War security debate has generated is an understanding that security is not a static and objective reality but is constantly shifting and incorporates changing ideas, perceptions and norms. Security is, in this conceptualization, as much a process as a concept and is deeply entwined with social and political dynamics.

This has certain methodological implications that have been explored through the concept of securitization (Buzan et al. 1998; Buzan 1999). The question that Barry Buzan and Ole Waever ask is how do particular concerns, whether political, economic or environmental, come to be generally recognized and accepted as 'security' issues? Their argument is that this comes through a process whereby certain actors successfully promote a certain issue as 'posing an existential threat to a designated referent object' which 'requires exceptional measures and/or emergency action to deal with it'. Security is not, therefore, understood as an end-point but as a process of securitization. This process is one which is highly political, in that such actors have to convince a wider audience of the appropriateness of designating that particular issue as a security issue. But it is also a process that seeks to go beyond the political in that the desired outcome is for the issue to be treated as a security rather than a purely political issue. The advantage of the designation of 'security' is that the particular issue is then accorded political priority and exceptional measures and the commensurate resources are then allocated for dealing with that issue. When understood in this light, it is not surprising that the concept of security has so clearly expanded and widened in scope as there is a clear political utility for this.

The concept of securitization is thus helpful for thinking about energy security. What it highlights is that there is nothing fixed or pre-determined about energy security; it is a dynamic and fluid concept which is a site of contestation for differing interest groups to claim their preferences for prioritization in relation to energy policies and to articulate preferences for what should have greater political salience. There is, thus, an eradicably political and politicized context for the study of energy security which includes both power struggles and differing ideological frames.

Energy Security and IR Theories

The fact that energy security is influenced by the particular normative and ideological frame that is adopted is, in fact, generally recognized in the literature on energy security. Most accounts make a distinction between a geopolitical or mercantilist conceptualization of energy security and a liberal, market-driven and pluralist approach. These two approaches map onto the classical divide in International Relations theory between realism and liberalism and can be fruitfully analysed as such.

The Realist Approach

Although a realist, geopolitical or mercantilist approach to energy security is sometimes depicted as old-fashioned and outdated, it has a continuing and enduring popularity and resonance. Arguably the most popular of academic writers on energy matters, Michael Klare, adopts a clearly, if not explicitly stated, realist framework. In his many books, the core overarching thesis is that the old ideological struggles between capitalism and communism of the Cold War era have now been replaced by a geopolitical struggle for access and control of valuable natural resources (Klare 2001, 2004, 2008). In contrast to the well-known argument of Samuel Huntington that the post-Cold War period is characterized by conflict between civilizations, Klare claims that 'it is resources, not differences in civilizations and identities, that are at the root of most contemporary conflicts' (Klare 2004: xii).

The reasons set out by Klare for this have classic realist foundations. He argues, first, that energy resources are vital ingredients of national power and prosperity and that states inevitably compete for access to these resources and are willing, in the final analysis, to contemplate military action. Dependence on energy resources is thus perceived as a source of national vulnerability. For Klare, it is natural that the fast-growing states of Asia, most notably China and India, are particularly sensitive about their dependence on energy imports and have adopted an increasingly mercantilist and geopolitical approach. Distrust and suspicion between the major consuming states is also exacerbated by the fact that the largest reserves of many of these energy resources are located in regions such as the Persian Gulf, Central Asia and Africa, where there are weak and fragile states with multiple internal and external sources of conflict, including political and religious extremism. With their increased resource wealth, these countries can potentially implode into civil wars, such as has been evident in many Sub-Saharan states, or adopt revisionist, anti-Western and authoritarian policies, such as in Russia, Iran and Venezuela. Although Klare does not suggest a direct causal link, he nevertheless sees a strong connection between oil and the emergence of transnational extremist Islamist groups such as al-Qaeda (Klare 2001: 82).

Klare's overarching realist-inspired thesis remains a powerful and persuasive framework which captures the political imagination of many analysts and policymakers. This energy security and resource dimension is clearly present in the broader dynamic of competition and conflict between the United States and China. For example, the growth of a Chinese presence in Africa and Latin America prompted US deputy secretary of state, Robert Zoellick, to accuse China of trying to 'lock up' resources and to claim that this had led to a 'cauldron of anxiety' around the world concerning China's geopolitical ambitions (quoted in Kessler 2005). The perception of Russia's energy stranglehold on Europe has similarly strongly influenced Western perceptions of Russia's policies towards Ukraine. Popular and elite discourse have also regularly resurrected the idea of a renewed post-Cold War 'great game' in Central Asia or a 'scramble for Africa' as part of a geopolitical struggle between China, the West and Russia over the oil, gas and mineral resources of these regions (Blank 1995; Karasac 2002; Frynas and Paulo 2007). The post-Cold War concern over resource-driven wars has also fed into this broader geopolitical anxiety. Influential research by Paul Collier demonstrated that most post-Cold War civil wars are not, as commonly assumed, caused by 'grievance' issues, such as ideological and identity claims, but rather by 'greed' and the material rewards offered in particular by control of valuable natural resources (Collier and Hoeffler 2004; Collier 2008).

The power and attraction of such realist-driven analyses reflect the enduring strengths of the realist tradition in International Relations. What the tradition does capture is the reality of an anarchical international system, a system lacking an overarching global sovereign authority, and the primacy of sovereign states as actors in the international system.

The Liberal Approach

The alternative liberal tradition has increasingly accepted this assumption of anarchy in realist thought. But where liberalism differs from realism is in asserting that realism presents only a partial and incomplete picture of the international system. Instead of a simple inter-state system, liberalism argues that the world is far more complex, pluralist and interdependent. In addition, liberals argue that realist policies and prescriptions, drawing from this only partial and limited understanding of political realities, actually undermines, rather than strengthens, international security and intensifies, rather than reduces, the prospect for conflict and war.

These two core liberal critiques of the geopolitical or realist approach are evident in the liberal anti-realist approach towards energy security. From the liberal perspective, a key flaw in the realist approach is its almost exclusive focus on states as the key actors in the international energy sector. This marginalizes or simply ignores the multiplicity of other actors, such as companies, regional and international bodies, and the variety of local and international non-governmental organizations (NGOs) and civil society groups. It also most crucially ignores the fact that most energy resources are developed, produced and processed by companies operating in a global market, which acts independently from the political realm. In reality, states intervene relatively rarely in these markets and are much more involved in establishing regulatory frameworks than in engaging in political or military interventions. For example, the international oil market is globally integrated and fungible and the historical trajectory is, if anything, towards enhanced transparency and openness to market forces. The development of the oil futures contracts and spot oil markets in London and New York has created a 'new oil world depending on short-term rather than long-term contracts' (Goldthau and Witte 2009a: 376). Global gas markets appear to be moving in a similar direction.

The liberal approach to energy security challenges realism by arguing that security comes through restricting, rather than expanding, the role of the state. From the liberal perspective, it is through accepting the complexity of the global energy systems and recognizing that states do more harm than good by intervening in these systems that an efficient, effective and thus secure international energy order can be constructed. Three liberal prescriptions are at the heart of this understanding of energy security. First, energy security is promoted through the expansion and strengthening of market forces, most notably through the deregulation, liberalization and privatization of energy markets. States continue to have a role in this process but this is limited to structuring and regulating the market and not through seeking to act as a privileged independent force or to supplant the market. Second, energy security is advanced through the enhancement of transparency and pluralism in policy making and in domestic and international institutional arrangements. This is ultimately fostered through a more pluralistic political system which, particularly at the domestic level, requires more open democratic practices and respect for human rights. A key tenet of liberal thought is that illiberalism at home promotes illiberalism abroad and some of the most significant sources of global energy insecurity are found in the illiberal practices of many resource-producing states. The third liberal prescription is the need to promote and strengthen regional and international institutions, which can help to mitigate exclusive state sovereignty and support international coordination and cooperation in the international energy sector.

The Radical Tradition

The liberal approach towards energy security is, like the realist account, a powerful and enduring framework for promoting a more secure global energy environment. Realism and liberalism map, to a certain extent, onto the division discussed earlier between traditional and non-traditional conceptions of security. While realist analyses focus primarily on the political and military dimensions of energy security, liberal accounts identify a much more complex array of actors and processes and the interdependence of modern energy systems. Instead of a world formed primarily of states, liberal accounts present a globalized market structure within which states interact with an array of actors, requiring a more pluralistic and interconnected approach operating with certain clear norms and practices. The more cosmopolitan framework within the liberal approach is also a key influence on the promotion of human security and how this incorporates the issues of energy poverty within the remit of energy security.

Much of the analysis of the rest of this book is influenced by the competing underlying realist and liberal theoretical approaches to energy security. These are powerful and enduring traditions which continue to frame the ongoing debates and discussions over energy security. However, there is a third tradition in classical International Relations theory that provides an alternative but also influential, if at times neglected, framework for understanding

the dynamics of energy security. This is what was originally called the Marxist approach but which is now more
broadly depicted as a Marxist-inspired radical or critical
approach to International Relations. The essence of this
approach is that it offers a critique of both realist and
liberal approaches, arguing that neither promotes a genuinely radical critique of existing unjust global structures
and practices. Realism is taken as almost to be self-evidently
flawed since its explanation of international behaviour
assumes no potential for radical change and thus explicitly
condones the structural injustices of the international
system. Liberalism is a more complex ideological challenge
as it does offer prescriptions for change and reform and
on principles which appear to be based on altruistic or
benign universal principles. But the radical critique is that
these liberal prescriptions actually only perpetuate rather
than challenge the underlying deeply unjust structures of
power and domination.

For classical Marxists, this is because liberalism defends
and supports rather than condemns global capitalism. For
the later Marxist variant of dependency theory, economic
liberalism represents an ideological justification of imperialism, consolidating rather than dismantling the domination of the North and the oppression of the South. For
more contemporary critical theorists, liberals are con-
demned for taking a 'problem-solving' approach, which
means relying on technical solutions to the resolution of
problems, rather than adopting a truly 'critical' approach,
which asks more profound questions of the moral and
political legitimacy of the contemporary international
system (Cox 1981). For example, radical green advocates
argue that it is liberalism's dogmatic commitment to economic growth and to global capitalism that is the underlying cause of the environmental crisis facing mankind.

The importance of incorporating this third more radical
tradition is simply that Marxist-inspired radical thought
has undoubtedly played a powerful role in the intellectual
and political struggles surrounding the energy industries.

For example, the history of coal cannot be understood without taking into account how coal miners, and particularly their representative workers' unions, were steeped in socialism and the radical tradition and sought radically to challenge the perceived injustices of the industry and of society more generally. The rise of OPEC in the 1960s and 1970s, and the energy security crisis that this engendered, can similarly not be understood without taking into account the context of a broader radical challenge of the South to continuing imperial Northern domination. In the Middle East and elsewhere, the linkage of oil with Western imperialism remains a popular and politically powerful force. Without this, the rise of resource nationalism and the re-nationalizations of the oil industry in Venezuela, Russia and Central Asia during the 2000s cannot be properly comprehended. The global energy industries continue to be high-profile targets of a variety of radical environmental, anti-globalization, indigenous peoples and other movements, which utilize a radical anti-systemic and anti-liberal ideological framework.

Energy Security as a Value

This third more radical tradition brings to the foreground the need to include considerations of justice in relation to the existing structures of political and economic power in the global energy industries. However, it is also important to stress that this justice dimension is only one element within a multi-dimensional conceptualization of energy security and is one which needs to be incorporated into a broader analytical framework.

One way to think about this is to recognize that energy security is a value and, though important as a value in itself, can only be properly understood in its relation to other core values which are essential to what Aristotle calls the preservation of the 'good life'. One widely used definition of security is as 'the absence of threats to acquired values' (Baldwin 1997: 13). Security is, in this sense, essential to the promotion of a harmonious polity as the reality, or the perception of the reality, of external threats to the values of a society creates fear and anxiety, undermining the prospects of a good life. However, security cannot be an absolute value because risk, contingency and competition are essential attributes of other values that societies hold to be just as important. For example, a market-based economy seeking to promote economic prosperity requires a highly competitive and risk-based framework that generates insecurity. In such economic systems, prosperity requires a certain amount of insecurity. To seek to promote absolute security would only result, as the Soviet Union ultimately discovered, in substantial economic losses.

The realist and liberal approaches to energy security can be seen as offering competing interpretations of the appropriate balance between these values of security and economic efficiency. In the realist analysis, energy security is about ensuring that the state's energy interests are protected through minimizing or neutralizing external economic, political or military threats. In the liberal analysis, energy security comes through promoting and institutionalizing the economic and political interdependence of global energy systems. From the liberal analysis, there is a positive correlation between more efficient and more secure energy markets and that it is possible to have both the benefits of economic growth and prosperity and security of energy supplies. From the realist perspective, there is greater scepticism that such a virtuous cycle can be guaranteed and that more specific state-directed policies to promote energy security need to be included.

Energy security is, thus, a value which competes with the value of prosperity and economic efficiency. This reflects the fact that the provision of security generally costs money and this raises questions of affordability. Another value which energy security increasingly competes with is that of sustainability, particularly in the light of the environmental challenges that climate change presents for the future evolution of energy systems and the need to make a transition away from dependence on fossil fuels. It is clearly not in the interest of society as a whole for energy security to be promoted if it results in the type of devastating environmental damage that exponential global warming would cause. Indeed, the need here to find a balance between the three values of energy security, prosperity and sustainability raises a number of complicated interconnected policy challenges. The radical question is how to move towards ensuring a sustainable global energy system which also provides both energy security and continued economic growth.

The inclusion of justice as a fourth value completes the picture (see table 2.1). It acts to ensure the inclusion of a grounded political approach and the need to address the inequalities of the structures of power which generate energy-related insecurities. The justice dimension also brings attention to the need to incorporate broader issues of legitimacy, which are central to a more comprehensive analysis of energy security.

Table 2.1 Energy Security and Theoretical Frameworks

Theoretical Tradition	Global Energy Framework	Conflict vs Cooperation	Key Values
Realism	States as dominant actors	Anarchical system tends towards inter-state conflict	Security
Liberalism	Multiple actors, including companies, NGOs as well as states	Potential for cooperation through interdependence	Economic prosperity
Radicalism	Structures of domination: North–South	Resistance and revolution	Justice Sustainability

Conclusion

This chapter started by addressing the question of the definition of energy security and noted the importance of sensitivity to the differing contexts of energy security; to the variation between the political and systemic dimensions, the energy security specificities of differing energy resources, and the difference between access to energy resources and to energy services. It then located the study of energy security within international security studies and highlighted how the main tensions and conflicts over energy security can be understood theoretically through the competing normative frameworks of realism, liberalism and radicalism. This revealed significantly different ways of conceptualizing energy security and how these generate national and international conflicts and tensions as well as providing opportunities for cooperation. At its heart, the chapter argues that energy security involves contestation and that this necessarily involves a political process where power and justice issues are critical and concerns over energy security inevitably compete with other core values – such as economic prosperity and sustainability. Such a political process and struggle over energy security can also only be understood as part of a broader historical development and it is this historical context that the next chapter addresses.

– 3 –

The History of Energy Security

History can be cut or presented in differing ways. In approaching the history of energy security, there are two potential historical narratives, reflecting the differing theoretical approaches discussed in the previous chapter. The first narrative is that of the path towards modernity and how the history of energy is about the transition from the limitations of human power in the traditional pre-modern agrarian economy to the exponential expansion of such power in the modern fossil fuel-based industrial economy. It is a radical, revolutionary and even heroic story about the transformation in the human condition and the overcoming of the resource constraints that had limited the development of all earlier civilizations (Sieferle 2001; Crosby 2006). It is a story of how, in the past, energy was scarce and expensive while now it is cheap and abundant. As a consequence, the human population has grown from one billion in 1800 to seven billion in 2015; the world economy is 120 times larger than it was in 1500 and most of that growth occurred after 1820 and especially in the period 1950–73; and how massive population growth has been combined with per capita income growing nine-fold (Smil 1994; McNeill 2000; Kander et al. 2014).

In this narrative of modernity, the history of energy security is a history of human prosperity and emancipation. This emancipation is most clearly visible in the fact that modern energy systems release people from the drudgery of endless muscular toil. In the 2000s, the average global citizen benefits from the equivalent of twenty 'energy slaves', meaning that all the modern energy services that are currently available, such as for heating, communication and transportation, are equivalent to the services provided by twenty human slaves (McNeill 2000: 15). In advanced modern post-industrial societies, the number of energy slaves for each citizen is considerably greater. Such economic emancipation has also been accompanied, at least among a significant number of the most economically advanced countries, by political freedom and emancipation. It is here that this narrative of modernity converges with liberal claims that there is causal linkage between economic and political freedom. Energy security is, from this liberal modernist perspective, intimately connected to the human advancement from poverty and political subjugation to prosperity and liberty. Energy insecurity is evident when this transition has been blocked or impeded.

The second historical narrative does not question the empirical record of the expansion of modern power through the energy revolution. But it does challenge the equity and fairness of the resulting economic and political conditions, highlighting the structural inequalities and the unevenness of global development. With a modern fossil fuel-based economy, power has accrued to individuals, social classes and nations and has generated much greater levels of relative inequality than was the case in the pre-modern era. The realist tradition highlights how access and control over key energy resources is a source of tension and conflict between states who are anxious about their relative power and security. The Marxist tradition identifies how social relations have become more alienated in the process of industrialization, with increased inequality between the owners of capital and labour. In international politics, such inequality is expressed in Western imperial and colonial expansion. The history of energy security is therefore intimately tied to the lived experiences of structural inequalities. At its extreme, it encompasses the reality of a poor person in Sub-Saharan Africa who is significantly poorer even than an average person in the pre-modern era and whose fate appears even more scandalous when so many benefit from all the services that modern energy systems provide. A further dimension of this critical narrative is the environmental costs of the expansion of a fossil fuel-based civilization with the endemic pollution and the damage and destruction of natural ecosystems that it has caused.

This chapter will focus on this more explicitly political dimension of the history of energy security, incorporating the linkages between security, power and justice which is the central theme of this book. The chapter has three sections, covering the *longue durée* from the pre-modern period up until the end of the Cold War and the start of the new millennium. The first section examines the history of energy security from the perspective of the pre-modern agrarian economy and the social, economic and political transformations that occurred with the first industrial revolution and the shift to the use of coal as the primary energy source. The second section examines energy security in what is sometimes called the second industrial revolution with the shift from coal to the use of oil and electricity. It is in this period that the particularly strong association of oil with energy security becomes defined. The third section analyses the energy security crisis of the 1970s, which involved a major re-distribution of power from the energy-consuming to the energy-producing countries. It is in this period that the concept of energy security gained a global and highly political resonance. This section concludes with how the challenge presented to the global political order from the 1970s was subsequently seemingly overcome and neutralized during the 1980s and 1990s. This will set the stage for the following chapter 4, which will examine the resurgence of international concerns over energy security from the 2000s onwards.

From the Pre-Modern to the Industrial Coal Age

To apply the concept of energy security to pre-modern societies inevitably involves a certain imaginative retrospection and a temptation to compare those societies with our own. If such a comparison is made, pre-modern societies would inevitably be seen to suffer from severe energy insecurity. But, when judged on their own terms, utilizing the resources and technologies available at the time, many pre-modern societies developed sophisticated and advanced civilizations where the quality of life compared favourably with many contemporary societies. One can see this in the enormous artistic achievements of such societies, whether these be the Pyramids in Egypt, the medieval cathedrals in Europe or the ancient Buddhist temples in Asia.

But what was inescapably the case for all pre-modern societies, wherever and whenever they might have existed, was the limitations and constraints imposed by an almost exclusive reliance on energy that was obtained from products of the soil. Wind and water power generation were only very inefficiently utilized and over 95 per cent of all energy came from vegetable products (Cipolla 1962: 45; Kander et al. 2014: 39). The real existential challenge facing pre-modern societies was the exploitation of the soil in the most efficient way so that it would provide the primary needs of heating and mechanical power. Heating relied on firewood and required large expanses of woodlands and forests. Mechanical power involved, for the most part, the muscular exertions of humans or draught animals and thus the key source of energy had to come from food. This also relied on efficient cultivation of the soil and required tracts of land, leading to a need to manage a balance between woodlands required for heating and agricultural land required for food production.

Land and labour were, therefore, the two principal constraints on pre-modern societies. The constraint of the limited amount of available labour was potentially alleviated through population growth but this ultimately came up against the limits of available land and the need to manage sufficient supplies of both firewood and food. The pessimistic prognosis of Robert Malthus in the early nineteenth century that population growth would always eventually be reversed through famine and disease was a broadly accurate assessment of the pre-modern agrarian economy (Malthus 2003 [1820]). Famines were an ever-present threat to all traditional societies. The real underlying problem was that there was only so much mechanical energy that could be supported through human and animal exertions and thus a limit to the productivity gains that could be generated. In this context, it was not surprising that slavery was such a widespread and common feature of pre-modern societies as it was one of the most effective ways to concentrate power and energy. Rulers and leaders had to rely on slavery, or similar social forms of repression such as feudal tutelage, so as to generate the surpluses that could provide them with their military and other requirements. But, as John McNeill (2000: 12) notes, this power still remained limited when compared with later generations as 'Ming emperors and the Egyptian pharaohs had no more power available to them than does a single modern bulldozer or tank captain.'

The social divisions in pre-modern societies were highly unequal. Only a very small elite, those wielding either the sword (the aristocracy) or the book (the clergy), were mobile, educated and engaged in pursuits, such as music or hunting, freed from constant back-breaking physical exercise. The vast majority of the population relied on the plough (the peasantry) and their lives were limited to a small locality, to a monotonous and physically arduous routine, and a daily struggle to ensure sufficient supplies of food and heating (Gellner 1990). There was, as a consequence, a significant degree of equality between those who were not part of the small elite. But even the most powerful of monarchs or emperors in pre-modern societies were also constrained by the amount of power they could exercise. They could generally intervene and use military force to seek to quell uprisings and challenges to their rule, but their capacity to control or manage the everyday lives of their subjects was much more limited. Michael Mann calls this constrained power projection, which was inevitably somewhat unpredictable and arbitrary, 'despotic power'; the more intense and pervasive power, 'infrastructural power', where leaders and governments could actually penetrate their societies, only became possible in modern economic and political systems (Mann 1993).

On a global level, different societies and civilizations were also not so greatly differentiated in terms of their level of prosperity and wealth. Comparatively, it was actually Europe which traditionally was more severely constrained in terms of land and population as its agriculture was generally less intensive than in Asia, whose wet agricultural zones had rice, maize and potatoes as their main products (Boserup 1965). Certainly, Europe did catch up significantly during the eighteenth century with innovative developments such as the new rotation systems in agriculture, the introduction of new crops and the opening up of new land through colonization (Pomeranz 2000: 116–208). But even at the beginning of the nineteenth century, China and India remained the global superpowers of their day and Europe was relatively poorer (Marks 2002).

However, it was in Europe, and more accurately in England, that the decisive breakthrough was made from the 'bottleneck of renewable energy to the infinite resources of fossil fuels' (Bairoch 1983: 403). A key aspect of this was the shift to the use of coal as the primary energy source rather than reliance on biomass (Wrigley 2010). England had actually become increasingly dependent on coal for a long time prior to the industrial revolution. As early as the sixteenth century, England suffered from insufficient forests and the need increasingly to use coal, particularly in the big cities such as London. There were complaints even in 1700 about the pollution this caused, with a traveller, Thomas Nourse, stating that due to the coal smoke in London, 'of all cities perhaps in Europe, there is no more nasty and more unpleasant place' (Freese 2003: 35). But the advantage of using coal was that it meant that England was relieved of one critical constraint on the use of the available land – the need to ensure sufficient and sustainable supplies of woods and forests for purposes of heating. It meant that England could have a larger population than would have been the case if it had had to expand indigenous forests to meet the demand for firewood.

The use of coal, therefore, provided a potential resolution to one of the key constraints, that of land. However, it was only with additional technological advances that the second major constraint – that of the limitations on the generation of mechanical power – could be overcome. The key to this was the invention and development of the steam engine, which finally meant that mechanical power was not just limited to human muscle or the very inefficient use of wind and water. What the combination of coal and steam engines provided was a much more efficient way of producing iron than was the case with the traditional reliance on wood charcoal. The expansion of iron production then had a knock-on effect in that it supported the expansion of coal production through permitting deeper mining. Even more crucially, the steam engine, combined with ample supplies of iron, led to the development of the railways which meant that coal and machines could be transported greater distances, more quickly and in much greater quantities. This in turn led to the increasing mechanization of what had earlier only been craft industries, the first of these being the textile industry (Sieferle 2001; Marks 2002). This was the essence of the industrial revolution as a revolution in terms of power and it is a process which continues to this day.

There are two major energy security implications that came from this social, economic and political transformation. The first is that the possession of ample supplies of coal, added to the technological skills and machinery to convert this into mechanical power, was now a key attribute for countries to become vastly more powerful than others. Countries that lacked such supplies, and did not have the capability to develop modern industries as a consequence, became almost completely defenceless against the enormous concentrations of power that fossil fuel-fired industrializing powers, such as those of Britain, the US, France and Germany, could project. For example, British steam-powered warships in the first Opium war in 1842 demonstrated their complete superiority over traditional Chinese junks, signalling a major shift in the balance of power (Headrick 1981). In Africa, local fighting armies were slaughtered by relatively small European infantry forces wielding modern rifles and machine guns. It is, therefore, not coincidental that the high period of European imperialism came with the expansion of power unleashed by the industrial revolution and that coal, with the coaling stations set up across the British empire, was a key resource underpinning European imperialism. This established a chronic energy insecurity amongst the energy-poor parts of the developing world which continues to feed into anti-imperialist and anti-Western ideological traditions. It also fed into the growing struggle between the imperial powers themselves, with the coal fields of France, Germany and Belgium being major sites of conflict and contestation, such as in World War I.

The second implication was the way in which coal mining became a significant source of domestic political insecurity. This was in a context where the balance of power in domestic societies mirrored the vastly increased inequalities developing between states. As Marx captured in his theoretical conceptualization of capitalism, the key difference between pre-modern and industrial systems is that labour becomes devalued relative to capital and that power and wealth now accrues to those who own the machines or factories rather than those who work in them. When labour depends on muscular exertions, then the labourer has a direct input and has some control over the process; when it is a machine which does most of the work, the role of the labourer is less important. Indeed, and as factory owners quickly found out, children could often be as productive as adults and much cheaper. The conditions of workers, therefore, deteriorated and the relative inequalities between workers and owners or managers grew significantly (Huber 2008: 108–10).

Coal miners were paradoxically a partial exception to this. Coal miners managed to maintain a significant degree of bargaining power as the work that they did involved high levels of skill and a degree of individual control over what they did (Goodrich 1925). There was, as a consequence, a strong resistance to any form of mechanization which would reduce this relative autonomy. Miners were also the starting point of what Timothy Mitchell calls 'dendritic networks ... with a single main channel', feeding multiple industrial processes from a unified network which needed to operate without interruption if the whole national industrial and commercial complex was to be assured (Mitchell 2009: 408). The key vulnerability of this complex was that the coal needed to be mined in sufficient quantities and then taken by rail to feed the energy needs of the industries concerned. By withdrawing their labour, particularly if coordinated with rail or ship workers, miners had a very strong bargaining position. By the late 1880s and 1890s, miners were increasingly inclined to use this power and the mining industry registered significantly higher levels of strikes than other industries (Arrighi and Silver 1984; Silver 2005). Miners tended to be the spearhead of more concerted efforts to promote general strikes. Miners' unions became powerful forces in all the major coal-producing states, contributing to unprecedented state interventions, such as improvement of welfare conditions in Germany and institutionalizing collective bargaining in France (Canning 1996; Podobnik 2006). Indeed, the birth and origin of the European welfare state was forged through the economic and political exertions of working people, the most prominent and active of which were the European miners.

For many states and governments, miners became synonymous with political contestation, revolution and threats to domestic security. In the United Kingdom this continued right into the 1970s and 1980s, when a series of miners' strikes represented major challenges to the authority of the government (Eley 2002). In countries like South Africa, the perceived threats posed by local miners remains a major domestic political issue (Wallace and England 2013).

From the Coal to the Oil Age

The history of energy security during the period of the coal-driven industrial revolution is, therefore, closely intertwined with the disparities in power that it generated. On the international level, the disparities between those countries benefiting from the exponential growth of coal-fuelled development and those who remained tied to traditional economies were greatly magnified. This was a major source of the structural inequalities in international politics which continue to be a source of resentment to this day. On the domestic level, coal-fuelled industrial development created new social tensions and conflicts between the owners of capital and the industrial proletariat. Coal miners were victims of this but also had a relatively stronger bargaining position compared to other industrial workers to promote their interests and to seek changes to their terms and conditions. Miners are, as a consequence, traditionally closely linked to radical politics, challenging the dominance of liberal economic and political ideology.

In understanding the shift from a coal to an oil age, this should not be seen as a radical discontinuous event but rather as a gradual shift in the relative importance of these fuels for national and global economies. Coal dominated the first industrial revolution in the nineteenth century and continued to be the most important fuel throughout the first half of the twentieth century. Coal has also continued to be a vital energy source and is still the fuel of choice for industrializing countries. The fast growth of both China and India has come through the expansive use of their substantial domestic coal supplies. For example, despite vigorous efforts to diversify and use other fuels, over 80 per cent of China's primary energy use remains supplied by coal (Andrews-Speed and Dannreuther 2011; Mathews and Tan 2015).

Oil only gradually challenged the dominance of coal. Oil first had a major impact in the United States where it took an increasing share from 1910 onwards at the expense of coal (see figure 3.1). The real breakthrough in global oil use came in the post-World War II period when cheap oil flooded Europe and other parts of the world. The expansion in oil was also broadly concurrent with the expansion of electricity which together were major factors behind the unprecedented increase in global development and living standards in the immediate post-World War II

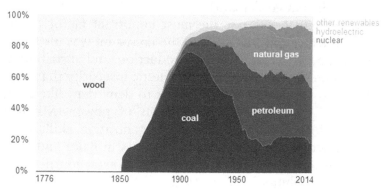

Figure 3.1   Share of Energy Consumption in the United States, 1776–2014
Source: US Energy Information Administration, Monthly Energy Review, 2015

period. Oil has an intrinsic advantage over coal in that it is a higher quality energy carrier and is, as a consequence, more energy efficient. In the same way as the coal age depended on the technological advance of the steam engine, so the oil age required its own distinctive technological innovation which was the development of the internal combustion engine. This innovative new engine was much more efficient than steam engines which were generally large and bulky; in addition, the most suitable fuel for these engines is petrol (gasoline), which has a higher energy density than coal and thus requires less fuel to be used. This was particularly an advantage for the most important invention to use the internal combustion engine: the car. It was really in the transportation sector that the oil age brought a genuine revolution as, with the car, mobility increased dramatically. People were no longer dependent on proximity to rail lines and could use cars, as well as planes, for business, home and recreational use. Oil also made shipping much more efficient and the subsequent reduction in transportation costs made oil itself cheaper to transport, leading to the development of very large oil tankers. The resulting reduction in the cost of oil meant that it was used increasingly to substitute for coal and further increased demand.

Although it was not the most important factor in the overall transition, the shift to the use of oil was also supported by the fact that its production and distribution represented a lesser threat to domestic insecurity than that posed by coal mining. This is not to deny that, like coal, oil gave workers some new forms of power (Mitchell 2011). Joseph Stalin learnt his organization skills as a young activist among Azeri oil workers in Baku and later reminisced that this had qualified him as a 'journeyman for the revolution' (Suny 1972: 373). The oil strikes in Baku in 1905, which contributed to the revolutionary turmoil in Russia, were followed by significant strikes of oil workers in Mexico in 1922, Venezuela in 1936 and Iran in 1945–6.

However, overall the incidence and success rate of strikes in the oil industry has been markedly less significant than for the coal industry. This is for two main reasons. The first is that oil production is generally much more capital- than labour-intensive as oil is not mined like coal but comes to the surface driven by underground pressures and thus requires a smaller workforce than coal. The second is that oil's liquid form makes it easier to transport than coal, and pipelines could replace railways and, though these pipelines are potentially vulnerable, they are not as easy to incapacitate through strike action as were the railways that carried coal (Mitchell 2009: 407). Moreover, once oil reached the coastline, it could much more easily and cheaply be transported by sea. Oil tankers, enjoying the freedom of the oceans, could avoid or circumvent political or other attempts to block their movements and, in addition, evade the labour regulations and democratic rights that coal miners had managed to obtain for their own industry. The substitution of oil for coal did, therefore, reduce the power of labour, in particular the power of the mining and transport unions, helping intensify capitalist development with less labour resistance. This was a significant element of its attraction as a fuel.

Oil has, though, one strategic vulnerability not present with coal: its deposits are considerably more concentrated, with the most abundant resources located in the Middle East. In contrast to coal, there is a significant disjuncture between the most important consumers and producers of oil. This is not so much the case for the two countries who became the most powerful states of the twentieth century, the United States and the Soviet Union, who both enjoy substantial domestic oil production. Their rise to power was certainly aided by this natural endowment, particularly for the Soviet Union whose model of autarchic economic development and territorial expansion would have been far more difficult to sustain without such abundant supplies of oil and, later, gas. But the traditional European great powers lacked such domestic sources and were more exposed to this new vulnerability and source of resource insecurity. This first became more clearly evident with the strategic decision of Winston Churchill, just before World War I, to convert the British navy into oil-powered vessels, thereby reasserting Britain's 'naval supremacy upon oil' (Churchill 1968: 529). Critics of this decision highlighted the dangers to national security of no longer depending on the coal fields of England and Wales but on the oil fields of an unstable Middle East, which one official called 'an old, long-mismanaged estate, ready to be knocked down' (Yergin 2011: 265).

The subsequent collapse of the Ottoman empire after World War I brought to the fore the critical energy security challenge of ensuring the uninterrupted supply of a vital resource whose most abundant supplies were located in foreign non-Western countries. This challenge generated two key responses and developments. The first was quite simply for the dominant Western countries to assume political and economic control of the Middle East, with pre-World War I rivalry replaced by a relatively ordered division of the region into spheres of influence controlled by Britain, France and the United States. Although the US eschewed formal imperial territorial control, Washington insisted upon an 'open door' policy, meaning that American oil companies were not to be denied access to the oil resources of the region as a consequence of imperial preferences or protectionism. It is here that the roots of the US commitment to a post-colonial informal liberal hegemony for global oil production and distribution can be found (Stokes and Raphael 2010; Ikenberry 2012). The decision to partition the Middle East cooperatively between the key Western powers, excluding defeated Germany and the communist Soviet Union, led to British, French and American oil companies dividing between them control over the major oil-producing regions.

This leads to the second major development: the devolution to these private Western oil companies of the responsibility for securing flows of oil from the Middle East. It was these companies who negotiated the terms of agreement with the key oil-producing states, such as Iraq, Iran and the Gulf states, which generally involved long-term, large-scale concessions favouring the interests of the companies over those of host states (Yergin 1991; Parra 2010). This devolution of power also involved a willingness by Western governments to overlook the collusive and oligopolistic cooperation of the major oil companies. The so-called 'seven sisters' ensured their control of the international oil industry through vertical integration of all stages of the value chain and by agreeing not to challenge each other through seeking a greater market share or by competing on price. Western governments' tolerance of such collusion was not just a question of political expediency to ensure control of Middle Eastern oil. It was also driven by the particularities of the oil industry, which is characterized by low short-run marginal costs and an in-built tendency to chronic overproduction leading to intense price competition (Stevens 2013: 15–16). If the production and price of oil of the relatively much cheaper Middle East had been determined by market forces, it would have meant that all other global production would have become uneconomic, including the domestic US oil industry, which was not in the US or Western interests (Luciani 2013: 124).

The end result of these two developments was that energy security was apparently achieved, at least from the perspective of the Western consuming states, for most of the mid-twentieth century. Oil was being produced in ever-larger quantities; it gradually displaced the less efficient use of coal; prices were low and stable; and oil fuelled the economic miracle of Western Europe and generated fast growth in many parts of the developing world in the 1950s and 1960s. The oil companies were both making exceptional profits and ensuring that the superficially 'free' market provided energy security. In retrospect, with the experience of the subsequent extreme volatility of oil prices, this may appear as a golden age of oil. In reality, this economic and political structure rested upon the political subordination of the Middle East's oil-producing states, the diversion of the share of economic rents from host states to the oil companies, and a lack of local control over these countries' core assets. Although the Western oil companies were the principal actors in terms of negotiating the contractual arrangements, they could always rely upon the coercive powers of their home states if there was significant resistance to the terms offered. This was most dramatically demonstrated by the CIA-engineered overthrow of the Iranian government of Mohammed Mossadegh in 1953, following local attempts to nationalize the Iranian oil industry (Yergin 1991: 450–78).

The First Energy Security Crisis

This essentially neo-colonial energy security governance, allied to a managed and oligopolistic global market, was eventually undermined by the success of the oil-exporting states, institutionalized through OPEC, in wresting economic power from the major oil companies. The resulting crisis, which dominated most of the 1970s, was when the concept of 'energy security' was first most fully articulated, gaining widespread popular resonance. The concept became indelibly linked to the feelings of insecurity generated by this epochal shift in the distribution of power from the oil-importing consumers to the oil-exporting states. In 1975, Henry Kissinger, US Secretary of State, dramatically recognized the nature of this shift and the West's relative weakness: 'the only chance to bring oil prices down immediately would be massive political warfare against countries like Saudi Arabia and Iran to make them risk their political stability and maybe their security if they did not cooperate. This is too high a price to pay even for an immediate reduction in oil prices' (Kissinger 1982: 674).

The causes of this shift were as much economic as political. First, the bargaining position of the oil-exporting states was helped by rapidly growing demand in Europe and elsewhere. Second, the cartelization of the industry was gradually being eroded by the rise of independent oil companies, many of them European state-owned national champions such as Italy's ENI. If there was a critical turning point in power relations between the oil companies and the oil-exporting states, it was in 1969 in Libya where the new leader, Muammar Gaddafi, successfully played off the majors and the independents to secure a significant increase in prices. The Libyan example was then closely followed by the Shah in Iran, demonstrating that this was not an ideological issue but rather one of a critical shift in the balance of economic and political power (Parra 2010: 152–4; Luciani 2013: 126–7). A third factor was undoubtedly more political: the growing assertiveness of the Third World, perceptions of declining US hegemony and growing antipathy to the US due to its support for Israel following the Arab defeat in 1967. In this context, the continuing presence and power of the Western oil companies appeared as a major derogation of the sovereign independence of the Middle Eastern states. It was this broader political context which led to the wave of nationalizations of foreign oil companies' installations, starting in Algeria in 1971, then Iraq in 1972 and Libya in 1973 (Seymour 1980: 218–30; Yergin 1991: 583–5; Aissaoui 2001). Unlike with Iran in 1953, there was no Western military response to these developments.

Although this power shift occurred prior to the 1973 Arab–Israeli war, it was this political crisis which led to oil prices increasing four-fold, thus reflecting the new economic reality. In popular and elite perceptions, it was the political and military dimension of the ensuing energy security crisis, most notably the exaggerated threat of the 'oil weapon', which appeared more evident than the underlying economic-induced shifts in the distribution of power. Such a politically charged understanding of the roots of the crisis was only reinforced by a second oil price spike following the 1979 Iranian Revolution. Henry Kissinger contributed to the confrontational response to the crisis by establishing the International Energy Agency (IEA) as a counterpart to OPEC, representing the interests of the Western oil-importing states. More cooperative producer–consumer dialogues were at times pursued, such as the Euro–Arab Dialogue, but did not develop any significant momentum.

Undoubtedly, OPEC's rise and the collective assertion of the power of the oil-exporting states of the Global South fundamentally disrupted the neo-colonial mode of energy governance which had characterized the pre-1970s global oil industry. However, it is important to recognize that this was only a partial reversal of the distribution of power in the international oil industry because OPEC crucially lacked the capacity to control the industry in the same way as the oil majors. OPEC's main weakness was that, while control over national production could be guaranteed, there was a more limited capacity to assert control over other parts of the value chain, such as refining, processing and distribution (Luciani 2013: 127). In reality, a key consequence of the end of the oil majors' hegemony was the undermining of the industry's vertical integration and its subsequent fragmentation into a mosaic of partly nationalized and partly liberalized and globalized sectors (Goldthau and Witte 2009a: 375–7).

Overcoming the First Energy Crisis (1980–2000)

This underlying structural weakness of OPEC provided the opportunity for the OECD countries to recover their strategic advantage. This involved three key aspects. The first was to encourage the international oil companies to compensate for their losses by diversifying production of oil and gas away from the OPEC countries and towards new oil fields in, for example, the North Sea and the Gulf of Mexico. The subsequent increase in non-OPEC production forced OPEC, especially Saudi Arabia, to reduce output so as to maintain control over the oil price. This ultimately became unsustainable, significantly reducing OPEC's power to set oil prices. The key shift occurred in 1985, when Saudi Arabia refused to play its appointed role as swing producer for OPEC, having had to reduce production from 10 million barrels per day to 2.2 million barrels per day, and increased the volume of its oil production. Accordingly, oil prices collapsed in 1985 to $13 a barrel (Parra 2010: 285–6).

The second part of the overarching strategy was to reduce dependence on oil by diversifying fuel sources, especially in the electricity sector. Although early hopes for nuclear energy to provide an infinite supply of cheap electricity failed to materialize, there was a turn to gas and, later, with rising concern over pollution and climate change, renewables like wind and solar energy. Accordingly, 'energy security' evolved: it was no longer simply linked to security of oil supplies, though these remained important, but included the broader, more complex question of the most 'secure' energy mix for a particular country, region or world as a whole (Stirling 2010; Cherp and Jewell 2011). Energy security thus shifted from being focused almost exclusively on the question of access to oil supplies, and the economic and political challenges represented by OPEC, to a more complex assessment of the overarching systemic requirements for energy systems which depended on a variety of different energy sources.

The third aspect was more political and involved the successful shift in power back to the West under US hegemonic leadership. Declining oil prices in the 1980s contributed to the political and economic weakening of oil-exporting states. The Iranian Revolution became mired in a long, bloody war with neighbouring Iraq from 1980 to 1988 and the US became a vital security guarantor for Saudi Arabia and the other Arab oil-exporting states. The Saudi–US alliance became a bedrock of energy security since, as the largest importer and exporters of oil, they shared a mutual interest in securing the global supply of oil at affordable prices. This relationship was cemented by cooperation in supporting the Mujahedin opposition to the Soviet occupation of Afghanistan. The decisive defeat of Iraq in the first Gulf War (1990–1), when Saddam Hussein attempted to gain control of Kuwait's energy resources, consolidated US hegemony over the region. The Soviet Union's subsequent collapse in 1991, due in part at least to the economic problems it faced with low international oil and gas prices, dissolved all challenges to US unipolar hegemony in the Middle East and other parts of the Global South. As Hinnebusch (2003: 218) notes, the 'collapse of East Bloc alternatives to capitalism and the end of Soviet patronage of Third World nationalism enormously increased the self-confidence of US elites that a capitalist Pax America could be imposed against lingering resistance in the Third World'.

The ideological counterpart to this decisive material shift in global politics was the dominance of a neo-liberal conceptualization of the international political economy. This had its roots in the ideological rejection of the Keynesian and socialist interventionist economic models which, it was perceived, had contributed to the economic crises and problems of the 1970s. This also had a clear energy dimension. It was the failure of the recycling of the surplus OPEC 'petro-dollars' to generate economic growth in many developing states, most notably in Latin America and Sub-Saharan Africa, which had contributed to the general economic crisis in the developing world. The indebtedness of these countries resulted in the North, through the IMF and World Bank, imposing structural adjustment programmes which demanded deregulation, privatization and economic and political liberalization. The significant drop in oil prices in the 1980s meant that Middle Eastern countries, including some oil-producing states, were not immune to such pressures and were obliged to implement their own economic liberalization programmes.

The ideological dominance of the neo-liberal model of economic governance had specific impacts on the oil and gas industries during the 1980s and 1990s. Most Western countries privatized their national oil companies and the market became more diversified and fungible, with an array of smaller oil companies and service companies competing ever more effectively with the international majors (Bridge 2008: 397–8). The financialization of the industry through the development of a futures market in oil spurred the industry's liberalization. The opening up of the previously autarchic Soviet oil and gas industry yielded new opportunities for private investors and the sector became increasingly controlled by a small number of Russian 'oligarchs', who were also generally open to Western investment (Luong and Weinthal 2010). An increasing number of other oil-producing states sought to limit the state's role in their resource sectors and to encourage Western companies to enter their markets (Moran 1998; Ramamurti 2001; Vivoda 2009). For example, in the early 1990s the Venezuelan government encouraged the national oil company, PDVSA, to become increasingly autonomous and to restructure itself along the lines of a Western private oil company.

By the end of the 1990s, many analysts suggested that the increasingly globalized and liberalized 'market' had essentially resolved the problem of energy security. The well-known oil analyst, Edward Morse, captured the mood, arguing that 'resource nationalism has practically disappeared from the discourse of international relations' (Morse 1999: 28). Oil was cheap, in plentiful supply, and some believed that low prices would last indefinitely, with the world on the cusp of an 'era of cheap oil' (Jaffe and Manning 2000). Accordingly, there appeared to be a consensus that natural resources should not be treated differently from other sectors of the economy, such as manufacturing, and should be liberalized, privatized and open to foreign investment to improve efficiency and productivity (Dietsche 2013). Intellectually, this was supported by the 'resource curse' thesis (see chapter 5), which appeared to provide conclusive proof, at least for many Western policymakers, that oil-exporting states which attempt to exert direct state control over their resource industries suffer from poor economic development, a tendency towards authoritarianism and the potential for violent conflict (Karl 1997; Sachs and Warner 2001; Ross 2012).

Conclusion

A number of the themes and issues raised in this chapter, such as the question of the 'resource curse', will be addressed in later chapters. The next chapter will also bring this story of energy security from 2000 to the present day and set out the reasons why concerns over energy security were revived, leading to what could be called the 'second' major energy security crisis. However, what is important to take from the standpoint of the late 1990s was that the dominant overarching energy security narrative appeared to corroborate the more optimistic liberal modernizing narrative that was presented in the introduction of this chapter. From this perspective, the first energy security crisis of the 1970s was a relatively short and ultimately failed attempt to challenge this benign trajectory, which was successfully reversed by developments in the 1980s and 1990s with the return to global economic growth and the expansion of political freedom. This was the period of the 'third wave' of democratization which culminated in the end of the Cold War and the collapse of the dominant alternative economic and political system represented by the Soviet Union (Huntington 1991). The key lesson appeared to be that the energy industry could support this progressive development if it was permitted to operate freely and was not unnaturally constrained by economic protectionist measures or geopolitical intervention.

The dominance of this narrative did not, though, fatally weaken the alternative energy security narrative which highlights how energy security needs to incorporate the structural inequalities and injustices that flow from the expansion and development of modern energy systems. From this alternative perspective, the energy security crisis of the 1970s successfully exposed some of the underlying inequalities and injustices of the way that the global oil industry had traditionally operated. Although this was certainly partially reversed in the following two decades, this reversal was not total and a key lesson was that energy security cannot effectively be assured unless the underlying structures of power and questions of international and social justice are addressed. For proponents of this view, the emergence of a new energy security crisis in the 2000s only confirmed their analysis.

– 4 –

Energy Security and Contemporary International Security

The late 1990s represents the high point of the counter-reaction to the social, economic and political legacies of the first energy security crisis of the 1970s. On the eve of the millennium, oil prices were at historic lows, even dropping to under $10 a barrel in 1998. The power of OPEC had been significantly reduced with the expansion of non-OPEC production. The major energy-importing industrialized states had, over the preceding period, developed a more diversified energy mix, expanding gas, nuclear and renewable energy, and thereby creating greater resilience against oil security shocks. Concerns over the environment, especially recognition of the negative impacts of climate change, increasingly came to dominate discussions over energy security, leading to greater emphasis on reducing, rather than expanding, the demand for fossil fuels. More generally, energy security was viewed as being best provided through the operation of more open and effectively regulated global energy markets rather than through state intervention and geopolitical competition.

The 1990s, the first decade after the end of the Cold War, was a period marked by Western confidence. There was a conviction that the intellectual and practical superiority of liberal democracy and capitalism had been conclusively demonstrated by the evident failures of alternative authoritarian and state-controlled political and economic systems. Francis Fukuyama captured this through his Hegelian-inspired reflection on the 'end of history' (Fukuyama 1992). This sense of Western dominance was materially manifested in the unrivalled power of the United States and the seeming lack of serious opposition to the expansion of Western liberal norms and institutions (Wohlforth 1999; Ikenberry 2001).

In terms of energy security, this ascendance was linked to the decisive overcoming of two serious challenges. The first was the collapse and subsequent opening up of the autarchic state-controlled energy sector in the former Soviet Union. During the 1990s, newly independent energy-rich states in the South Caucasus and Central Asia opened up their previously tightly closed territory for exploration by a variety of external foreign actors, including private Western investors, fuelling what some came to call a 'new great game' in the region. Within Russia itself, the state divested a significant portion of its control over the oil and gas sectors, allowing new local and foreign private players to gain control over these resources (Gustafson 2012). The second challenge that was overcome was more conservative in its nature. This was the large-scale Western intervention to enforce the withdrawal of Iraqi troops from Kuwait after the invasion of that country by Saddam Hussein in 1990. The liberation of Kuwait in 1991 ensured that US power and hegemony was enhanced through strengthening the most important bilateral relationship for energy security – the US–Saudi compact (Dannreuther 1992; Freedman and Karsh 1994).

However, this particular political and economic order, which appeared to entrench the dominance of the West, was to be short-lived. Political resistance and new power configurations emerged surprisingly quickly, which fundamentally challenged the liberal optimism of the immediate post-Cold War period. In terms of international energy politics, the confidence of the 1990s was challenged by the return to an energy security crisis that had parallels with the 1970s. As in that earlier period, the most concrete expression of this renewed concern was the soaring cost of oil which reached its peak in 2008 at a price of $147 a barrel, though subsequently, in response to the global recession starting in 2008, falling back to around $100 and then, in 2014, dropping precipitously to below $30 a barrel. Similarities to the 1970s were also evident in the linkage between heightened global energy security concerns and political instability in the oil-rich Middle Eastern region, most notably with the rise of Islamist extremism, the terrorist attacks by al-Qaeda on the United States in 2001 and the US-led invasion of Iraq in 2003.

There were, though, two further dimensions to this renewed anxiety over energy security that had not been present in the 1970s. The first was the inclusion of a number of non-Western emerging states as key energy consumers who had, or were at least perceived to have, an approach to energy security that was significantly more interventionist and geopolitical than the Western norm. Particular suspicions and concerns in this regard were directed towards China, whose very active and global energy diplomacy to ensure secure supplies of oil indicated a significant shift in the global political balance of power (Andrews-Speed and Dannreuther 2011). The second new dimension was the revival of an empowered and increasingly anti-Western Russia who, unlike the Soviet Union, was more integrated into global energy markets and was more willing to incorporate energy politics into its broader challenge to a Western-dominated international order (Newnham 2011; Kuzemko 2014).

This chapter analyses these three contemporary geopolitical dimensions (Middle East, China and Russia) to energy security, bringing up to date and completing the history of energy security which was covered in the previous chapter. The focus on energy security in the contemporary period also offers a critical insight into the complex interconnection of energy security with international security. While there is no crude causal linkage between energy security and international conflict or war, there are nevertheless myriad ways in which developments in international security are deeply interpenetrated with anxieties over energy security. As the larger thesis of this book argues, energy insecurity is intimately linked to shifts in the balance of power and in the associated claims for justice and equity. In the following three sections examining the interconnection between international politics and energy security in the Middle East, China and Russia, the issues of power, resentment and injustice are powerful drivers, influencing and contributing to many of the energy-related tensions and conflicts in these regions. The chapter concludes with the implications of the significant fall in oil prices in 2014 and whether a new regime for energy security, resembling more the period of the 1980s and 1990s than the 1970s, might be developing.

9/11, Energy and Persian Gulf Security

The Middle East is the natural starting point for approaching international energy security since the region is deeply politically and militarily volatile while also vital for global energy supplies. The Persian Gulf region constitutes not only a critical 28 per cent of world oil production but also holds close to 50 per cent of the world's oil reserves and, primarily due to Saudi Arabia, over 70 per cent of excess oil productive capacity. As in the past, the Middle East holds the main concentration of proven oil reserves globally (see figure 4.1). It is also the excess capacity that provides Saudi Arabia with the strategic capacity to be the 'swing producer' and to be able to influence global supply that no other producing state can rival (Nakov and Nuno 2013). It was the potential threat to this key source of international power that made Saddam Hussein's invasion of Kuwait in 1990 appear such a critical threat to

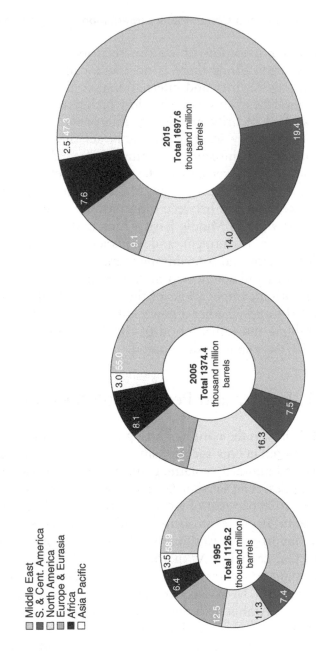

Figure 4.1 Distribution of Proved Oil Reserves, 1995, 2005 and 2015
Source: BP Statistical Review of World Energy 2016

international security. The large multinational composition of the UN-sanctioned coalition to liberate Kuwait, including over 50 countries, demonstrated the unprecedentedly high level of international consensus behind the military intervention to counter Iraq's hegemonic ambitions in the region (Dannreuther 1992; Lieber 1992). This action also illustrated the capacity of the US to assert and maintain a hegemonic position in the region and was broadly supported by the other key Western powers, such as Germany, France, Britain and Japan (Bromley 2005; Stokes and Raphael 2010). This intervention was also passively supported by the Soviet Union (as it was still then), China, India and most other developing countries.

This unusual degree of international solidarity provided a brief period of optimism for the political development of the Middle East. Significant efforts were invested in a drive to resolve the Arab–Israeli conflict which resulted in the Oslo Accords between Israel and the Palestinians initially agreed in 1993 and which was followed by an Israeli–Jordanian peace settlement in 1994. Saddam Hussein's Iraq was greatly weakened, sanctions were imposed, and the country no longer represented a serious threat to regional order. In Iran, the death of Ayatollah Khomeini in 1989 opened the way for a more moderate leadership under the presidencies of Akbar Hashemi Rafsanjani (1989–97) and Mohammad Khatami (1997–2005) and the gradual, if limited, liberalization of domestic society and economy. In other countries in the Middle East, there was a similar movement to greater liberalization, if not democratization, with moves particularly in the economic sphere permitting a greater role for the private sector (Hinnebusch 2006; Zubaida 2012).

However, even during the 1990s, the underlying sources of instability and political fragility were evident. Islamist politics moved away from directly challenging the principal Middle Eastern regimes, which had only resulted in increased repression, towards assuming a radical pan-Islamic and anti-Western ideology focused on a global jihad. The growth of al-Qaeda as a political movement reflected this shift away from the 'near enemy', meaning the local Arab dictatorships, to the 'far enemy', meaning the West and the United States (Gerges 2005). The political ideology of this new strain of Islamist politics was what Oliver Roy termed 'neo-fundamentalist' in that it rejected classical notions of the secular nation-state and promoted an order based on the exclusive moral prescriptions of Shari'a law (Roy 1994, 2004). The threat that al-Qaeda represented to the West was its commitment to international terrorism and its willingness to countenance mass casualty terrorist acts. The subsequent attacks in 2001 on the Pentagon in Washington and the World Trade Center in New York brought home the existential gravity of this emerging threat to international security.

Western strategic anxieties also increasingly focused on the key revolutionary states in the region – Iran and Iraq. The catalyst for these fears was the growing sense that both Iran and Iraq were determined to develop weapons of mass destruction (WMD), including a nuclear capability. In Iraq, this concern was driven by the failure of the sanctions regime to get Iraq to comply fully with the UN mission to oversee the destruction of all of Iraq's WMD. As a consequence, there was a growing perception that Iraq was hiding its WMD programme. In Iran, there were similar fears over the country's nuclear ambitions, which were confirmed by the revelation in 2002 that it was secretly engaged in a nuclear enrichment programme in contravention of its nuclear non-proliferation treaty (NPT) obligations. Both Iran and Iraq were, as a consequence, incorporated into the category of so-called 'rogue states', who represented fundamental challenges to the international system and who could not be treated as normal civilized states (Litwak 2000). President George Bush even called them, along with North Korea, part of an 'axis of evil' in his State of the Union speech in 2002.

This mix of international terrorist, radical Islamist and WMD proliferation threats resulted in two major US policy strategic initiatives. The first was the dual containment policy which imposed sanctions on both Iran and Iraq during the 1990s. This meant a large-scale US military presence in Saudi Arabia and among the other small Arab Gulf states. This policy articulated the understanding that there was no realistic opportunity for either Iran or Iraq to be integrated fully into the regional and international economy without a fundamental change in their domestic and foreign policies. Although not all external powers fully subscribed to these policy prescriptions, and Russia and China were either ambivalent or opposed to them, the strategy of containment meant the imposition of significant political and economic costs on both Iran and Iraq. The second policy initiative was the much more radical decision in the aftermath of the 9/11 terrorist attacks to intervene militarily in both Afghanistan in 2002 and Iraq in 2003 so as to impose regime change in both countries.

Both policies had significant implications for international energy security. The policy of dual containment involved the use of the 'oil weapon' in reverse, initiated and implemented by consuming rather than by producing states. The clear determination of the US and its allies was to restrict and limit not only the export of oil and gas from Iraq and Iran but also to limit the development and expansion of their energy sectors. This led naturally to a restriction of the supply of globally available oil which in turn had an impact on oil prices, contributing to their rise during the 2000s. It is a rarely noted paradox that arguably the greatest political obstacle to the expansion of oil production during this period was not the recalcitrant behaviour of the oil-producing states but rather the US sanctions policy on two of the world's major producers (Van de Graaf 2013).

The deliberate isolation of Iran also had major longer-term regional energy security implications. During the 1990s, one of the most dramatic developments in energy politics was the emergence of Central Asia as a major new energy-producing region. There was much excitement among analysts about the emergence of a new 'great game' which pitted Russia against the United States and other regional powers (Blank 1995; Karasac 2002). However, the one option that the Central Asian states could not realistically pursue was the one which was economically by far the most logical and efficient – to develop the infrastructure to supply global oil and gas markets through the territory of, or through partnership with, Iran. This was because the sanctions policy on Iran made it impossible to obtain the investment necessary to develop the infrastructure for making energy linkages through Iran. The exclusion of these prospects meant that they had either to continue to remain dependent on Russia or to develop much more expensive and politically contentious energy routes to Europe or to China.

The energy security consequences of the decisions to intervene militarily in Afghanistan (2002) and Iraq (2003) were more diffuse and less easy to quantify. However, what can be said is that these interventions led to significant shifts in the regional and international balance of power, which in turn revealed a series of historical injustices and resentments which, as the central theme of this book argues, contribute to growing energy insecurity. In terms of the international balance of power, the immediate post-9/11 period was one of the US administration feeling both radically more vulnerable and yet also more convinced of its capacity to change the world through democratic transformation (Dorrien 2004; Callinicos 2005). In both Afghanistan and Iraq, there was an initial expectation that both countries would be transformed into liberal, pro-Western countries which would become catalysts for economic and political reform in the rest of the region (Tripp 2002–3; Dannreuther 2013: 219). The subsequent failure of US and Western state-building efforts in both countries, and the rise of powerful resistance movements which greatly increased the costs of occupation, contributed to the decline in the prestige and relative power of the United States and the West. As the next two sections of this chapter explore, this has increased the relative power of other major actors, such as China and Russia, who have themselves had much greater influence in the contemporary period on the international politics of energy than had previously been the case.

In terms of the regional politics of energy security, the most significant impact of the occupation of Iraq was in its contribution to shifting the balance of power in the region. Overthrowing Saddam Hussein meant also the overthrow of the Sunni-dominated minority regime which had controlled political power in the Iraqi state since its formation after the collapse of the Ottoman empire. The resulting empowerment of the long repressed Shi'a majority paradoxically meant that the US invasion had contributed significantly to the strengthening of Iran's political influence in the region. With Iran already influential in Lebanon through its alliance with the Shi'a political force, Hezbollah, and being tied politically with the non-Sunni Alawite Syrian regime of Bashar al-Assad, Sunni perceptions of the threat posed by Shi'a Iran significantly increased. This was particularly the case with Saudi Arabia, and an intense rivalry and mutual suspicion developed between Iran and Saudi Arabia, which in turn created tensions in relations between Riyadh and Washington. The enflaming of tensions between Sunni and Shi'a and other minority communities in the region contributed also to the strengthening of radical Islamist forces, most notably the radical Islamist and terrorist group Islamic State (ISIS), which gained control over significant parts of Iraq and Syria (Gerges 2016). Overall, the resulting political situation in the Middle East was of recurring deep instability and conflict which meant continuing anxieties over ensuring energy security.

It is a mistake, however, to make a simple causal linkage between oil and conflict in the Middle East or to understand US policy in the region as being driven solely by its resolve to control the region's oil resources. There are, in reality, multiple sources of conflict in the Middle East that are more linked to the injustices generated by the region's historical state formation process rather than to the struggle for oil – the Arab–Israeli conflict is the most notable example of this. The United States also has multiple reasons for being heavily involved in the region beyond its interest in securing oil, including its support for the defence of Israel, its economic interests including arms sales, and its global strategy promoting counter-proliferation and counter-terrorism.

However, the fact that the Middle East does possess abundant supplies of the most valuable energy resources undoubtedly has an impact on regional and international security. Regionally, the unequal distribution of oil and gas resources within the region generates internal tensions and resentments. When oil wealth combines with revolutionary change and a powerful sense of historical injustice, this does contribute significantly to heightening tension and conflict. As Jeff Colgan has demonstrated, revolutionary petro-states are more prone to war than revolutionary non-petro-states (Colgan 2012). The Iran–Iraq war (1980–8) and the Iraqi invasion of Kuwait (1990) are examples of this regional proneness of a combination of oil resources and revolutionary ideology to lead to militarized conflict. This issue is developed further in the next chapter on the resource curse.

Oil also does not provide a sufficient explanation for the presence of external powers in the region. However, the energy resources of the region undoubtedly does help to explain the intensity of the interest of external powers and the degree of competition between them. The Middle East is distinguished by being, as one author has expressed it, more 'penetrated' than other regions due to the sheer number of competing external powers and that this accentuates and exacerbates internal tensions and conflicts in the region (Brown 1984). The example of the differences between the United States and Russia, as well as Turkey and Iran, over how to resolve the Syrian civil war, particularly concerning the role to be played by President Bashar al-Assad, is an example of a merging of internal and external politics which complicate and intensify conflict in the region. Overall, it is the strategic importance of the global dependence on the energy resources of the Middle East that drives this intense external interest in the region. The frequently competitive and interventionist nature of this external interest contributes in turn to the overall instability of the region and thus to global energy insecurity.

Energy Security and the Rise of China

The 2003 Iraq war was the moment when the US was at its peak in terms of internal and external perceptions of its power. At that time, there were few who doubted that the United States was the most powerful state in the international system. Where there was some debate, it was about whether the US was simply unrivalled and unchallengeable, a unipolar power, or whether it was one power, if undoubtedly the most powerful, among a number of powers in a multipolar system (Wohlforth 1999; Ikenberry 2001). What was rarely articulated at that time was the sense that China was a serious contender to challenge US hegemony. However, within only a few years, it was almost taken as axiomatic that China was a 'rising power' with the capacity not only to challenge but also to catch up with the United States (Mahbubani 2008; Zakaria 2008). In global debates and discussion, there was a clear shift from seeing the US as the sole superpower to the depiction of a multipolar world and even to considering a potential duopoly with China. This shift was, certainly, in part due to the difficulties faced by the US in Iraq and Afghanistan, as noted in the previous chapter; but it was also the result of a period of unprecedented fast economic growth within China during the 1990s and 2000s.

Energy played a significant role in highlighting and accentuating China's rise. Until 1993, China was a net exporter of oil; since then, its demand for oil has grown steadily and inexorably. Net imports of oil reached 150 million tonnes in 2004 and then doubled to 300 million tonnes in 2012 and are projected to rise to 400–500 million tonnes in 2020. In 2006, China became the world's largest emitter of greenhouse gases; in 2012, China surpassed the United States as the largest energy consumer; and in 2013 it became the world's largest energy importer. The shattering of these records is a clear indicator of the extraordinary fast export-oriented growth which made China into the world's global manufacturing hub. From 2002 to 2012, China's primary energy consumption almost trebled; in contrast, in the US and the EU consumption stagnated or even slightly declined. China's fast growing demand for energy was itself part of a broader pattern of the emerging economies of the South, rather than those in the industrialized North, as almost the sole sources of future demand for global oil and gas resources. In geo-economic terms, this represents a significant shift in international energy trade away from the West and towards the East and particularly towards China (see figure 4.2 for the relative shift from the OECD countries to Asia from 1971 to 2014).

In the energy security crisis of the 2000s, China therefore played a role which was radically different from the 1970s when its influence was non-existent. China's economy was not just a significant factor behind the increase in global demand for oil but China was also now one of the largest consuming states which, like other consuming states, had to confront the challenges of energy security fears. But China did not fit easily into the existing Western governance structure of consuming states which adopted, under US leadership, a broadly compatible and cooperative energy security approach. Although there was clearly a certain convergence of interests between China and the other Western oil-consuming states, China was not permitted or interested in joining the International Energy Agency (IEA) as it was not a member of the OECD. China's non-Western identity and its authoritarianism and opposition to liberal pluralism provided significant obstacles to more

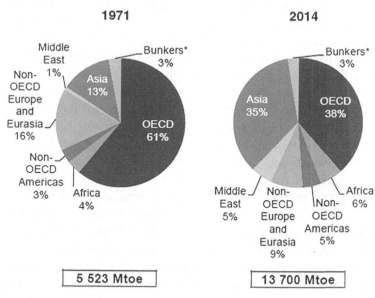

*Including international marine and aviation bunkers

Figure 4.2   Total Primary Energy Supply by Region, 1971 and 2014
Source: © OECD/IEA 2016 Key World Energy Trends (Excerpt from world energy balances), IEA Publishing. Licence www .iea.org/t&c

substantive cooperation (Friedberg 2005). This feeds into Western perceptions of China's international energy policies, with concerns that China has generally adopted a neomercantilist strategy to gain control of global oil supplies through privileging relations with anti-Western energy-rich countries. In 2005, for example, US Deputy Secretary of State Robert Zoellick accused China of seeking to 'lock up' energy supplies and alleged that there was a 'cauldron of anxiety' in the US and other parts of the world over Chinese intentions (quoted in Kessler 2005).

China's global search for supplies of oil did change the international politics of a number of regions and often significantly enhanced the bargaining power of emergent energy-rich countries. A good example of this is

Sub-Saharan Africa where China has actively sought to gain access to African oil supplies, most notably in Sudan and Angola, as part of an expansive economic and diplomatic engagement with the continent. This Chinese presence provided African states with the opportunity to diversify their external relations away from the previous almost exclusive dependence on the West and, with growing global demand for oil and other commodities, to have greater opportunities for mutually beneficial trade and development (Downs 2007; Brautigam 2009). A similar trajectory can also be seen in Latin America where the fast expansion of Chinese trade and investment in the region similarly benefited the economies of the region and permitted them to diversify away from their dependence on the US market (Palacios 2008; Ratliff 2009). In Central Asia, China's economic engagement, driven in large part by its oil and gas interests, has likewise helped these countries to reduce their dependence on Russia and to diversify the destinations of their energy exports (Laruelle and Peyrouse 2009). Indeed, there is practically no part of the world which has not been affected by the surge of growth in China and this, just in itself, has changed the content and substance of global energy security.

The larger question is whether this greatly increased presence and influence of China in global energy markets has had a significant destabilizing impact on international politics and global governance. The fear that China might seek to translate its increased economic power projection into a sustained geopolitical challenge to the West is generally understood to be exaggerated. In Africa, Latin America and the Middle East, China has generally not sought to challenge directly US hegemony and power. Where China has had differences with Western policies, these have tended to be expressed through quiet diplomacy and symbolic opposition and have been much less vocal than, for example, Russian criticisms. Chinese leaders and analysts have also increasingly realized that a neo-mercantilist approach to energy security is counter-productive and economically and politically expensive (Downs 2004; Houser 2008; Andrews-Speed and Dannreuther 2011). Chinese oil companies have often just sold their equity oil in international markets rather than shipping it back to China. In addition, the government has also become increasingly aware of the reputational damage caused by some of the activities of these companies, as they have been accused of failing to meet the standards of behaviour expected of international companies with respect to labour conditions, safety and environmental considerations (Ziegler 2008). Indeed, the Chinese government and oil companies have come to accept that they are not immune from the political risks facing other Western companies and thus need to work cooperatively with both external and internal stakeholders to ensure a stable investment environment (Moreira 2013).

However, there are also limits to the extent to which China's energy security approach converges with that of Western countries. There is, first, the fact that Chinese oil companies are different in form and nature from the model of the Western international oil company. They are state-owned, powerful and autonomous actors who are able to benefit considerably from the political and diplomatic support provided by the Chinese government. They have access to finance through low-interest loans from the state-owned banks and generally do not have to pay dividends to the government as shareholder. The Chinese oil companies can also offer attractive development packages to the target countries, offering support for large-scale infrastructure projects in exchange for access to oil and other resources. Critically, also, these agreements do not generally include demands of political conditionality, making it possible for China to engage with 'pariah' states such as Sudan, Iran and Venezuela.

There is, as a consequence, an understandable fear among Western companies that when they have to compete with the Chinese, they are not operating on a 'level playing field'. While the extent and degree of this competitive advantage is difficult to gauge, what can be said is that the growing Chinese engagement in the global energy markets has contributed to the general move away from the liberal agenda of the 1980s and 1990s and the resulting rise of resource nationalism and a more state capitalist model for the oil and gas sectors (Bremmer 2008; Bremmer and Johnston 2009; Dannreuther and Ostrowski 2013: 113–14; Belyi and Talus 2015). This raises also a broader issue of concerns that China might be 'free-riding' on the public goods in relation to energy security provided by, for example, US naval investments to ensure security of sea-lanes and the pricing security provided by the establishment of oil stocks provided by the IEA (Olson 1965). To be fair, this is a recurring issue in intra-Western debates, such as over burden sharing for NATO and European security, but these concerns have become even more prominent with the rise of emerging non-Western Asian states such as China (Olson and Zeckhauser 1966; Hartley and Sandler 1999; Sandler and Shimizu 2014).

The second main constraint is that, as China increasingly factors its energy security concerns into its diplomatic and military strategies, this is bound to create new tensions and potential conflicts, if only indirectly and sometimes unintentionally. Militarily, the perception of the Chinese oil imports being vulnerable to interdiction or blockade along the sea lines of communication (SLOCs) from the Persian Gulf to the Chinese mainland, most notably at the Malacca Straits, has contributed to the political objective of developing a blue water navy, something that the People's Liberation Army (PLA) Navy has itself promoted through emphasizing the need to protect energy imports. This has, in turn, generated concerns among Indian analysts and policymakers where they have interpreted Chinese engagement in the Indian Ocean as a 'string of pearls' strategy, whereby investments in the ports of Kyaukphu in Myanmar, Chittagong in Bangladesh and Hambantota in Sri Lanka are viewed as part of a deliberate longer-term ambition to displace Indian power (Pehrson 2006). The influential commentator, Robert Kaplan, has followed the logic of this and argued that the new centre for international conflict in the twenty-first century is likely to be the Indian Ocean and precisely for this mix of economic and political competition (Kaplan 2009). There is, for example, the potential for military escalation in the South and East China Seas where the presence of possible significant energy reserves intersects with competing territorial claims and inter-state rivalry. Although the Chinese government has emphasized how the opportunities for joint development of these energy resources should help to generate cooperation and trust, there is no evidence that this has actually led to territorial compromise. Indeed, as China's power and influence have grown, so its military, diplomatic and political stance on these territorial claims has appeared to become harder and more intransigent.

Energy Security and the Return of Russia

The example of China illustrates how shifts in the balance of power, in this case the increase in the power of China as an energy-consuming state, create their own dynamics and tensions which challenges existing structures and paradigms of energy security. It is important to emphasize that these shifts can potentially lead as much to enhanced cooperation as to conflict. As argued above, China's approach to energy security has shown a general move away from a narrow neo-mercantilist to a more multilateral and market-oriented understanding of energy security. Experience in countries like Sudan and Libya, where Chinese investments in their energy sectors have suffered from internal conflicts, has also demonstrated that the Chinese government cannot be completely disinterested in issues of political governance. However, even if there are signs of convergence, these are balanced by the fact that China's new strategic importance has radically changed global energy politics. Indeed, China's international search for securing reliable energy sources is an integral and critical part of the overall

Chinese rise as a great power and thus an integral part of the challenge that this presents to the international system and the existing global status quo.

Russia's contribution to the changing dynamics of energy security is similar in that Russia has also gained in power and influence since the early 2000s. Like China, but more openly and overtly, Russia has increasingly expressed its dissatisfaction at the Western-dominated international order, culminating in the most serious challenge to that order with the annexation of Crimea in 2014. Indeed, China and Russia have increasingly converged in their fundamental normative understanding of international relations and have significantly enhanced their political, economic and military ties with each other (Ferdinand 2007; Duchâtel and Godement 2016). During the 2000s, Sino–Russian energy relations developed positively with a number of oil and gas agreements, including a breakthrough agreement in 2014 for Russia to build a pipeline and export gas to China. There are clear mutual interests for both Russia and China in developing their bilateral energy relationship (Lo 2008; Dannreuther 2011: 1353–8). For China, Russia provides a vital component of its overarching energy security strategy since energy coming from Russia is not threatened by the United States as is the case with oil or gas coming from the Middle East, Africa or Latin America. For Russia, China is a very important new market for its energy exports which can potentially compensate for political strains with the West and thus alleviate the effects of economic sanctions and reduce over the longer term its economic dependence on Europe.

However, the big difference between Russia and China is that the former is a major energy-exporting rather than an energy-importing state. While China is representative of the fast-growing import-dependent emerging countries, including states like India and Turkey, Russia follows the pattern of a number of energy-exporting countries, such as Iran and Venezuela, who have come increasingly to adopt an anti-Western political approach and have promoted a form of 'resource nationalism' (Bremmer 2009; Vivoda 2009). For Russia, the reliance on its energy resources as a major vehicle for its strategic and geopolitical ambitions is actually quite new. While energy certainly played a role in the Cold War confrontation between the Soviet Union and the West, it was generally quite marginal to this conflict. The Soviet Union was self-sufficient in energy and the principal foreign policy function of its energy supplies was to subsidize the satellite countries of Eastern Europe in exchange for political loyalty. Although there were Western fears of potential Soviet intervention in the Persian Gulf so as to cut off Western energy supplies, there was never any serious threat of this nature. Indeed, it was in the energy sector that the most significant example of economic and political cooperation between the Soviet Union and the West was developed. The development of the vast Soviet gas resources in northwestern Siberia in the 1970s and 1980s was very much a joint project, where the Soviet Union provided a reliable source of gas for European markets in exchange for the Western technology and expertise to build the pipelines and compressor stations required to transport that gas. The Soviet Union actually went to very considerable lengths to insulate these Soviet–European energy relations from broader geopolitical developments and to thereby demonstrate its reliability as an energy supplier (Hogselius 2013).

The question is, therefore, why post-Soviet Russia would change from this traditional strategy of reassurance, generating considerable anxiety in the EU and its member states concerning the security and reliability of Russian energy supplies. One reason for this is the legacy of the privatization of the Russian oil industry during the 1990s. This had resulted in the concentration of economic and political power among a small number of oligarchs who controlled a large part of the energy sector. Domestically, this process was popularly viewed to be flawed, illegitimate and contributing to the political corruption and perceived economic and political failures of the first decade of post-Soviet rule (Gustafson 2012). With Vladimir Putin becoming president in 2000, a decisive shift took place when one of the most successful private oil companies, Yukos, was taken over by the state in 2003 and the company's CEO, Mikhail Khodorkovsky, was sentenced to a long period in prison (Thompson 2005; Sakwa 2008). This initiated a process of increased state control over the oil industry, conforming to the control which had never been relinquished in the gas industry, and the assertion of the political primacy of the state over all other actors, including powerful economic interests (Goldman 2008; Locatelli and Rossiaud 2011; Bradshaw 2014: 105–15). This move to assert state control was generally popular, particularly given the rise in oil prices during this period, and was part of a general pattern of increasing centralization of power and the development of a more authoritarian and repressive political regime. As such, Russian energy policy, much like its political development, was going in the opposite direction to the liberalization agenda of the European Union and this created friction and generated mutual suspicions (Kryshtanovskaya and White 2009; Kuzemko 2014). The Russian refusal to ratify the European Charter Treaty, which was the main EU initiative to address its energy security concerns in relation to upstream investment and transit, reflected this increasing ideological and practical divergence.

A second factor was how post-Soviet Russia under Putin, in contrast to the Soviet practice, focused increasingly on energy as a key resource to support Russia's great power status. The 2003 Russian energy strategy stated that Russia's energy sector 'forms the basis for its economic development and an instrument for its internal and foreign policy'. In 2005, Putin clearly articulated that Russia needed to be a leader in global energy and thus indirectly supported the widespread and popular conceptualization of Russia as an energy superpower (Baev 2007; Rutland 2008). The perceived political utility of Russia's energy resources contributed to the decision for the state to regain overarching control of the industry. Energy also became used as part of a broader Russian strategy towards those neighbouring states who might be tempted to move closer to Europe or to the United States, either through the EU or NATO. This came in a number of forms: threats of suspension of supplies of gas, changes in the pricing for those gas supplies, and aggressive attempts to gain control over energy assets in these countries. In practice, the effectiveness of using these geo-economic tools to change or influence policy among Russia's neighbours has generally proven to be limited (Orttung and Overland 2011; Smith Stegen 2011). Russia has itself struggled with the geopolitical rationality of the subsidization of gas prices as against the economic rationality of maximizing returns. Russia also has its own legitimate interests to defend. In the various Russian–Ukrainian disputes, Russian policymakers have had to find a way to respond to Ukraine's consistent failure to pay for the gas that it has used and, when supplies are as a consequence suspended, to appropriate the gas destined for European markets. But, wherever the fault might lie, the consequence of the two major gas disputes between Russia and Ukraine in 2006 and 2009 has been to increase significantly European energy security concerns towards Russia as a reliable supplier.

Another dimension to this geopolitical use of energy by Russia has been, as already mentioned, the power it has given potentially to balance against Western dominance. As relations with the West have deteriorated, particularly since the imposition of sanctions after the annexation of Crimea, so the strategic value of enhancing relations with China has increased. The main economic attraction of Russia for China is its energy resources which can ensure secure supplies not under threat from a hegemonic US presence. The finalization in 2014 of a major gas deal between China and Russia was a significant indicator of this Russian 'pivot to the East'. However, as with the geopolitical uses of energy in Russia's European neighbourhood, the reality does not match the public rhetoric of a fundamental shift in the global balance of power. China only agreed to this gas deal when it could assure a price which was competitive in domestic markets and which is generally recognized to be less than the gas price Russia sells to Europe. Both China and Russia also ultimately cannot afford to, nor wish to, risk their key economic partners in the West; Sino–Russian trade dropped from $90bn in 2014 to $64.2bn in 2015 and this bilateral trade remains a fraction of China's trade with the US or Japan or Russia's trade with Europe. Also, most of the gas that will flow to China will come from gas fields in East Siberia and not from fields in West Siberia, which supply the European markets. It is unlikely that Russia will ever be in a position to be able truly to balance its gas exports between China and Europe and, thus, its dependence on Europe will remain structurally embedded.

More generally, Russia also has a delicate relationship with the European Union that it needs ultimately to nurture and preserve since it is continued access to European energy markets which is absolutely critical to Russia's economic fortunes (Belyi 2015; Aalto 2016). Certainly, Russia has sought to weaken and divide the EU by privileging bilateral relations; it has resisted successfully the EU's attempts to extend its liberal regulatory regimes onto its own territory, such as refusing to sign the European Charter Treaty; it has also expended large financial and political capital on developing gas pipelines with the aim of increasing European dependence on Russia (Youngs 2009). However, even if the EU is properly understood as a liberal actor in energy policy terms, it is not powerless and, as Goldthau and Sitter (2015) argue, it is fully aware that, in an increasingly realist world, it needs to develop 'soft power with a hard edge', using the powers that come from its regulatory power and its capacity to deny access to the internal market. The actual real power of this can be seen in the way that it has successfully engaged in significant strenuous negotiations with the Russian gas monopoly, Gazprom, to ensure that its behaviour conforms with EU competition rules. The EU has also at times openly adopted a more geopolitical stance by supporting, for example, the Nabucco pipeline as an alternative to the Russian-sponsored South Stream. In general, Russian ambitions as an 'energy superpower' need to be balanced by recognition that it is the 'hidden' structural power of the EU market, with over 500 million people, where the real magnet of power lies.

Conclusion

The principal argument of this chapter is that the recent period has been characterized by a level and intensity of anxiety and concern over international energy security that has not been evident since the 1970s. The major oil- and gas-producing region of the Middle East experienced a level of conflict, external intervention and disintegration that is unprecedented even within the region's conflict-prone history. While the US-led invasion of Iraq was not primarily driven by oil, there was nevertheless a strategic objective to bring stability to the region which would enhance global energy security. The reality that the very opposite occurred raised the levels of concern and anxiety, particularly among Asian countries such as China, but also others like India, which are becoming increasingly exercised about their energy security given their fast-growing import dependence. The pace at which China, as well as other Asian countries, have become serious actors in oil-producing regions in every corner of the world has changed the geopolitical map of global energy security. As a result, the main oil-consuming states are no longer limited to the West, as was the case in the 1970s, but include fast-growing post-colonial and non-Western states who have differing perspectives and approaches to international energy security.

The experience of Russia and its economic and political strengthening with increasing opposition and tension with the West is also something seen among other energy-producing states. Like Russia, many oil-exporting states benefited from higher oil prices and translated this into domestic and foreign policies that have challenged the international status quo. In Venezuela, Hugo Chavez implemented a 'Bolivarian revolution' with radical populist and anti-American policies. In Iran, the radicalism continues to be based on the revolutionary Islamist doctrines that have guided the country since 1979. In Russia, the centralization of power under Putin sought to return Russia to the great power status that it lost with the collapse of the Soviet Union and which is seen to have been caused by a deliberate Western strategy to weaken and emasculate the country. What is common to all these cases, and is evident if in less stark forms in many other oil-producing countries, is that the shift in the balance of power in their favour has been accompanied by an accumulation of perceived historical injustices and a sense of continuing inequities that have often promoted confrontational and divisive domestic and international policies. These have naturally had an impact on the level of international anxiety and concern over global energy security.

In 2014, the international energy context did, though, change significantly when oil prices dropped from over $100 to $60 a barrel and then dropped further in 2016 to under $30 before recovering above $50. It is unclear as of late 2016 whether this is a temporary drop and prices can be expected to rise again or whether this relatively low price is likely to be more durable and to be sustained over a longer period. However, what can be said is that the substantial fall in the price of oil has put considerable internal pressure on the major oil-producing states. For countries like Venezuela, which failed to invest its oil gains in a sustainable manner during the 2000s, the collapse in prices has created enormous domestic social and political tensions and conflicts. More generally, for all revisionist states, the problems of external confrontation with the West are now matched by challenges of maintaining internal security and stability as the domestic economic situation deteriorates. Indeed, for all oil-rich states, including those in the Persian Gulf region, the shift to lower prices means a significant change in the balance of power, with an immediate challenge of managing a worsening domestic economic situation. This highlights the fact that energy security is not just about inter-state relations; it is also a critical dimension of the domestic politics within states. Just as issues of power, history and justice suffuse relations between resource-producing and resource-consuming states, so these factors are also embedded within the social, economic and political relations inside resource-rich states. It is this complex intra-state and domestic arena of political contestation over energy security which is examined in the next chapter.

− 5 −

Energy Security and Domestic Security

The previous chapter explored the multiple ways in which anxieties over energy security contribute to international insecurity, intensifying current conflicts in the Middle East and increasing antagonism and suspicion between the West, China and Russia. A widespread and popular argument is that a major factor behind this is found in the domestic failures and insecurities of energy-rich states. The political analyst, Thomas Friedman, developed this into a 'first law of petro-politics', which asserts that the higher the price of oil, the more authoritarian, anti-Western and rejectionist the majority of oil-rich states become and that this is a major factor behind the increase in conflict in the international system (Friedman 2006). It is, in effect, the presumed illiberalism of the oil-rich states that challenges and seeks to undermine the Western-dominated liberal international order (Wenar 2016). It is particularly at times when oil prices are high, and when oil-rich states can afford to assert themselves, that domestic and international conflict increases.

The so-called 'resource curse' thesis is the principal theoretical foundation for this focus on the domestic sources for insecurity and intra-state conflict among resource-abundant states. The thesis has three main strands to it (for overviews, see Rosser 2006; Stevens et al. 2015). The first is the economic argument that resource-abundant countries have simply failed to develop as effectively or as successfully as resource-poor countries, despite all the comparative advantages that resource wealth should bring. The second is the political argument that, in general, resource-rich countries are particularly resistant to democratization and tend to remain authoritarian, repressive and unequal. The third is an extension of this political strand and asserts that resource-rich countries are vulnerable either to implode and generate internal civil strife or to export their radicalism through engaging in violent conflict with other states.

This chapter assesses the resource curse thesis and its argument that resource wealth, particularly of fossil fuels, generates internal domestic insecurities and conflicts which undermine the security both within and between states. The first part of the chapter qualifies this argument by highlighting the well-known historical cases where resource wealth has undoubtedly contributed to successful economic and political development. There is, therefore, no inherent reason why resource abundance should not be considered a 'blessing' and, indeed, the traditional economic argument is that such resources should be considered as a positive contribution to enhance development. However, the incidences of developing states that have successfully used their resource wealth to diversify and develop a dynamic and balanced economy are relatively limited in number. The underlying reason for this is essentially political – the possession of valuable resources does not in itself support broader development goals unless combined with mutually reinforcing social and political institutions and practices.

The second part of the chapter assesses those resource-abundant states where the resource curse does apply as a significant factor. This first requires greater clarity on what is meant by the notion of the resource curse and to strip it of some of its more deterministic and fatalistic dimensions. The key insight is, again, that it is not the discovery or possession of these resources which in itself leads to developmental failures but the absence of the necessary social and political institutions and practices to ensure such positive outcomes. This is particularly relevant for post-colonial, developing states which lack the strong state identities and synergistic state–society relations that are present among the developed, industrialized states. It is not surprising, in this regard, that much of the initial focus of the resource curse is on the resource-rich states of the Middle East and Latin America, where the process of state formation has been divisive and often incomplete. The notion of the 'rentier state', originally defined in relation to the resource-rich Middle Eastern states, is a significant contribution to analysing why many countries with resource wealth have often failed to diversify their economies and have entrenched and consolidated social, economic and political inequalities.

The third part of the chapter extends this analysis to an understanding of the causes of violent civil and internal conflict linked to the struggle for resources and which has emerged as a source of growing concern in the aftermath of the end of the Cold War. This chapter argues that high levels of domestic violence and civil conflict among resource-rich states occur when there is a failure among elites to reach an agreement on the distribution of the resource rents and the resultant intra-elite struggle for access to these resources leads to violence. However, again, it is not the resources themselves that generate this conflict. There have also to be deep-seated grievances between the different groups over the relative injustices of the distribution of the resource wealth for that violence to ensue. Frequently, this will have a regional dimension with the resource being, for example, concentrated in one or more peripheral regions, and it is the perceived lack of legitimacy of the division of the benefits between the centre and periphery which ultimately generates the conflict.

Overall, the main argument of this chapter reflects the overarching argument of this book. Energy-related domestic insecurities, like the international insecurities discussed in the previous chapter, are fundamentally politically driven and relate to the perceived justice or injustice of the distribution of power determining the allocation and distribution of the benefits of the resource wealth. Among developed and developing states, the social and political conditions are such that there is a capacity to utilize the energy inputs for the broader benefits of society and the economy, though this is always continuously negotiated and contested. However, among more patrimonial and praetorian states, there is a tendency towards the exploitation and predation of the resource wealth which generates inequality and relatively poor economic development. In extreme cases, where there is a complete breakdown of social consensus, such as in failed or failing states, access to and control of such resources becomes a source of violent conflict.

Resources as a Blessing

Classical economic theory and mainstream development economics generally support the view that mining for natural resources is beneficial and should not be considered a 'curse'. The theory of comparative advantage, adapted from the work of David Ricardo and developed by Eli Heckscher and Bertil Ohlin in the 1920s and 1930s, concluded that a country should export commodities for which there are relatively abundant production factors. The export of such commodities was the comparative advantage of the country (Graulau 2008: 136). It was this idea of comparative advantage that was implicitly used to justify the specialization of European colonial territories in mining and extractive outputs. In the 1950s and 1960s, it was the Canadian staple theory that first applied comparative advantage theory in a rigorous and systematic fashion to minerals, mining and development. This body of research sought to explain the mainly positive role that natural resources historically played in the development of the Canadian economy (Innis 1956; Watkins 1963).

The staple theory stated that economies with an abundant supply of accessible natural resources have a meaningful advantage in the development process and that 'rapid progress in new countries is dependent upon the discovery and development of cheap supplies of raw materials' (Mackintosh 1964: 13). The important underlying assumption of staple theory is that natural resource exports should become the leading sector of the economy and set the pace of economic growth. Crucially, economic development is driven by a process of diversification around the export base. The central concept of the theory is the 'spread effects of the export sector, this is, the impact of export activity on the domestic economy and society' (Watkins 1963: 143). These spread effects include various forms of backward, forward and fiscal linkages to the rest of the developing economy. Forward linkages refer to the processing of the resource prior to export which, in the case of oil and gas projects, implies the supply of oil and natural gas products. Backward linkages refer to the inputs into the economy in terms of employment, capital and material inputs, such as machinery and infrastructure. Fiscal linkages refer to the revenue generated for the owner of the resource and involve the expenditure of the rents and profits generated by resource production (Gunton 2003: 68; Ostrowski 2013).

This generally optimistic view is a strong and continuing tradition in development thinking. In the immediate postcolonial period, staple theory converged with modernization theory, viewing the prospects for external investment and assured access to foreign markets as being a major advantage for resource-rich developing countries, providing them with an opportunity to integrate faster into the global economy and to move from a lower to a higher stage of development (Rostow 1960). During the period of the commodities boom from 2000 to 2014, the mood was similarly positive, viewing the extractive industries as a source for broad-based development for resource-rich developing countries. Such positive outcomes were not viewed as automatic but critically requiring 'good governance', involving, *inter alia*, respect for the rule of law, strong institutions that implement regulatory reform and enforce laws, revenue and contract transparency, and the effective use of stabilization funds to smooth revenue volatility (Stevens et al. 2015: 18–19). Many developing countries, including those from Africa, were seen to have substantially taken on board these requirements and were now benefiting from their often new-found resource wealth (Luciani 2011). In a foreword to the 2013 annual report of the Africa Progress Panel, the UN secretary-general Kofi Annan noted that 'defying the predictions of those who believe that Africa is gripped by a "resource curse", many resource-rich countries have sustained high growth' (Africa Progress Panel 2013: 6).

This overarching tradition of economic thought, which sees resources as a potential blessing, is a necessary corrective to a fatalistic or an overly deterministic view of resources always having negative consequences. There is substantial historical evidence of resource wealth leading to and promoting economic development and growth. As discussed in chapter 3, the early industrializers, such as Britain, Germany and the United States, used their supplies of coal and other mineral deposits as key inputs into their development process. Ample supplies of coal were certainly a pre-condition for the industrial revolution that first occurred in Britain. But it is also important to note that it was not a sufficient condition for such a radical economic transformation. It was only when the steam engine was developed that the coal supplies could then be transformed into iron production, which then combined to lead to the development of the railway network and supported the increased mechanization of industry, starting with the textiles industry (Sieferle 2001; Marks 2002).

Similarly, it was not oil as a physical resource on its own that independently fostered the industrial transformations of the twentieth century. Just as coal depended on the technological advance of the steam engine, so the oil age required its own technological innovation which was the internal combustion engine. It was this that transformed individual and collective transportation with the development of the car, plane, and petroleum-fuelled sea shipping.

As is highlighted in staple theory, it is the capacity for resources to promote forward and backward linkages and to advance the diversification of the economy that is critical for socio-economic development. For this to happen, though, requires a capacity for technological innovation and scientific knowledge which can promote these broader goals. David and Wright illustrate this in the case of the United States by arguing that its historical achievement of industrialization cannot be reduced to its fortunate resource endowment (Wright 1990; David and Wright 1997). Rather, it was the social and intellectual capital underpinning resource extraction in America that was critical, including the ability for 'collective learning, a return on large-scale investments in exploration, transportation, geological knowledge, and the technologies of mineral extraction, refining and utilization' (Wright and Czelusta 2004: 10). It was, therefore, not the natural endowment in resources which ultimately explains the striking industrial advances, and ultimate economic hegemony, of the United States, but the accommodating legal environment, the investment in the infrastructure of public knowledge and the provision of education in mining, minerals and metallurgy. It was this which gave the United States its comparative advantage and also provided the scientific and social basis that drove the broader manufacturing revolution.

The US example of successful resource-based development can also be seen to be mirrored in later developing countries. Norway is one oft-cited example. From being a peripheral and structurally undeveloped country in the 1960s, Norway utilized its oil and gas discoveries to reorient its traditional engineering skills in shipbuilding towards gaining international expertise in advanced oil-producing technologies, such as producing deep-water drilling platforms. Through supporting scientific knowledge, Norway not only expanded its oil reserves but also made its indigenous companies significant players in the international oil industry. Overall, Norway successfully managed to diversify its economy away from dependence on oil production while accumulating huge financial reserves.

However, even though Norway was a relatively poor European country prior to its oil discoveries, it had a long-established democracy with effective political institutions and a history of low levels of corruption. In addition, it had developed skills in shipbuilding and extensive experience of working at sea which greatly facilitated developing its mainly offshore oil deposits. Examples of resource-rich countries which lack such histories of state cohesion and democracy and yet have also been successful in developing their 'resource blessing' are harder to identify. The developing countries most frequently cited in having made a particular success in using their resource wealth are Chile, Botswana, Indonesia and Malaysia. Given the very significant differences between these disparate states in terms of size, regime type and histories, it is not easy to identify common sets of factors behind their relative successes. However, one element evident in all of these states is the role played by a competent and economically qualified bureaucratic administration, protected and relatively autonomous from the political domain, which was capable of pursuing a long-term set of developmental objectives for their respective countries (Stevens 2006). Each of these states had generally long-lived governments that were strong either through democratic support or by military control (Booth 1995; Tsie 1996; Shamsul 1997; Hojman 2002). In the cases of Indonesia and Malaysia, the regional context was also one of the 'Asian miracle' which bucked the trend in the 1980s in successfully promoting fast economic growth. There was, thus, an extent to which these countries followed a broader regional pattern of development.

Indeed, a significant part of the attraction and popularity of the resource curse theory was precisely the contrast in the 'lost decade' of the 1980s between the fast growth in East Asia, and specifically among the resource-poor 'Asian Tigers', as compared to the sluggish and unimpressive growth in the resource-rich countries of the Middle East and Latin America. It was this comparison which appeared to corroborate the view that resource wealth might be the key factor that constrains economic growth while resource poverty encourages such growth. However, in the same way as the mere presence of natural resources cannot explain the relative success of the four resource-rich developing countries cited above, so the fact of a lack of such resources does not adequately explain the success of the resource-poor Asian Tigers. The principal factors behind the success of these Asian countries, resource-poor as well as resource-abundant, include strong and cohesive state and national identities, a powerful and developmentally minded set of bureaucratic elites and a supportive geopolitical context (Cumings 1987; Stubbs 1994, 1999). It is when these factors are lacking or more limited among other countries that such countries, including resource-rich countries, struggle to translate their resources into a dynamic, durable and diversified economy – this is the key insight, when properly contextualized, of the resource curse theory.

Resources as a Curse

The idea that resource abundance might be a constraint on development is closely associated with the historical experiences of resource-rich regions in the developing world. The first substantive critique of the positive view of extractive industries was linked to the experience of Latin America in the interwar and immediate post-World War II period. The very difficult economic conditions in the region led a number of social scientists to question whether the integration of Latin American economies into international markets had been beneficial. The Argentinian economist, Raul Prebisch, was the leading figure in this intellectual movement and he offered a structuralist critique of how the theory of comparative advantage did not produce positive results in Latin America (Prebisch 1950, 1963). He argued that there was a structural constraint for those regions in the 'periphery', where the international division of labour meant that they specialized in the production of raw materials, while the developed industrialized countries specialized in manufactured goods. The problem was that, contrary to the theory of comparative advantage, those specializing in agriculture or mineral commodities were structurally disadvantaged due to the long-term decline in the terms of trade for raw materials exports (Singer 1950). This meant that in effect their national incomes declined over time and their failure to diversify, particularly into higher value-added manufacturing, locked them into a cycle of weak or negative economic growth.

Prebisch's key insights on structural international economic inequality provided the basis for the development of the dependency school of thought, which again had a strong Latin American dimension. This school developed further the core–periphery elements of the structuralist theory to identify the ways in which the international division of labour perpetuated the condition of underdevelopment of the periphery (Baran 1957; Dos Santos 1969; Furtado 1970). These include the negative political development of a 'dualistic' system where there is a division between the masses engaged in the subsistence economy and the elites, drawn from the pre-capitalist feudal and landowning classes, who join with foreign capital to develop the export-oriented agricultural and mineral economies. The consequence is not just the underdevelopment of the economy but also a regressive and unjust social and political division between local elites and wider society and an overall domination of the country by foreign monopolistic capital. For leading dependency theorists, such as Paul Baran, foreign mining or oil companies were the quintessential manifestation of the exploitation and domination of such foreign monopolistic capital (Baran and Sweezy 1966).

The policy prescriptions which followed from these structuralist and dependency critiques were generally protectionist and nationalistic. To break the cycle of underdevelopment, it was believed necessary for the national state to assume control over the major export-oriented industries and to use the resulting rents to diversify the economy through import substitution industrialization. The more radical critiques also included the need to promote a social and political revolution to break the power of foreign capital. Latin American countries were the first developing countries to nationalize their oil industries: Mexico in 1938 and Brazil in 1953. To this day, the tradition of protectionism and the desire to reclaim national sovereignty against foreign domination remains a powerful one. Private Western oil companies have gained a particular reputation as the agents of foreign and imperialist exploitation. The populist social and economic policies pursued by Hugo Chavez and his successor in Venezuela, with similar movements in Argentina and Bolivia, are evidence of the continuing power and attraction of this tradition.

The main problem with these policy prescriptions, however, is that in practice they did not resolve the 'resource curse'. This should, though, be qualified by recognizing that politically, Latin America remains distinctive, compared to other resource-rich regions like the Middle East and the post-Soviet countries, in that there is no clear correlation between resource wealth and authoritarianism. Indeed, it was during the resource boom of the 1950s that Venezuela became a democracy, followed by other countries including Ecuador and Bolivia. Dunning argues that oil actually hastened democratization by alleviating the concerns of wealthy elites that democracy would lead to expropriation of private wealth (Dunning 2005). However, economically, the resource curse does apply as the prescriptions did not result in the economic development expected. The problem, as clearly evidenced in Mexico, was that the subsidization of the infant industries through the rents obtained in the oil sector singularly failed to lead to a globally competitive industrial sector. These industries remained dependent on continued subsidies, thereby critically starving investment in the oil sector. The result was that Mexico was particularly marked by the resource curse to the extent that by 1982, as Auty pointed out, 'virtually the entire non-oil economy became non-tradable, i.e. in need of total protection or subsidies' (Auty 1994: 22). A similar resource-related economic story can be told about Venezuela (Karl 1997).

The fact that a similar pattern of frustrated economic development also emerged in the Middle East in the aftermath of the oil boom of the 1970s prompted a new paradigm for understanding the peculiarities of oil-abundant states. This was the concept of the rentier state (Mahdavy 1970; Beblawi 1987). The key insight of the rentier state theory is that rents from the oil production are derived externally, go directly to the government and 'only a few are engaged in the distribution or utilization of it' (Beblawi 1987: 51). The rentier state is, in Luciani's description, an 'allocative' rather than a 'productive' state, relying on the unearned income from the externally generated rents rather than on the extraction of resources from productive economic activity through taxation (Luciani 1987: 69). The consequence of this is that these rents provide a significant degree of autonomy of the government and state elites from other social forces and groups. This means pressures from below for reform and social and political change can either be 'bought off' through the distribution of material benefits or can be 'silenced' by a security apparatus paid for by external rents. This leads to the stagnation and ossification of political regimes, such as the traditional monarchies among the Gulf states, characterized by patron–client, neo-patrimonial networks and repressive authoritarian structures.

The resultant rentier state is intrinsically ill-suited to dealing with the significant economic challenges which come from dependence on oil and gas resources and the need to move towards a more diversified economy. There are three particularly difficult economic challenges identified in the resource curse literature that need to be addressed (Sachs and Warner 1995; Auty 2001; Rosser 2006; Stevens et al. 2015). The first is the need to overcome what is called the 'Dutch disease', which refers to the experience of the Dutch when they discovered and produced gas in the 1950s and how this led to a contraction of the non-oil economy, particularly manufacturing, due to the appreciation of the real exchange rate. Understood more broadly, the notion of the Dutch disease identifies the real difficulty of ensuring that the oil sector does not make the other sectors of the economy less competitive due to the way in which it draws human and capital resources from these other sectors (Fardmanesh 1991). As noted above, the strategy to protect such non-resource sectors, such as manufacturing or agriculture, through subsidies generally just exacerbates the problem.

The second challenge is linked and relates to the 'enclave' nature of the oil industry, which refers to the fact that the industry tends to be highly capital-intensive, to require limited labour inputs and to be geographically limited or isolated. The core problem is that there tends, as a result, to be limited backward and forward linkages to other sectors of the economy (Hirschman 1958). This contrasts with manufacturing industry where such linkages are more present and where dynamic linkages between different economic activities are generally developed. In many oil-rich countries, the oil industry is an isolated and autonomous sector with very limited interaction with other economic activities or the rest of society.

The third challenge, which exacerbates the management of the previous two, is the volatility of natural resource prices, particularly oil. The average change in oil prices since 1970 has been 26.5 per cent (Ross 2012: 51). Volatility of such magnitude makes prudent fiscal policy difficult, tends to exacerbate investor uncertainty and increases the potential of windfall gains being used for consumption rather than investment (Mikesell 1997; Luciani 2011; Saad-Filho and Weeks 2013). Without effective stabilizing measures, it is difficult for governments to resist political pressure to spend on the domestic economy when the going is good and to cut spending when there is a fall in oil prices, leading to the accumulation of debt. In good times, resource-rich governments frequently develop an informal contract with civil society that compensates for the lack of political freedom with the promise of economic prosperity. However, this contract becomes increasingly strained when prices and revenues drop, such as with the recent oil price slump, and these governments find it increasingly difficult to 'buy their way out' of rising domestic tensions. This is most vividly seen in Venezuela where the profligacy and economic mismanagement during the period of high oil prices has led to subsequent economic chaos, violence and deep instability as the oil revenues have declined.

The typical rentier state finds it particularly difficult to manage these complex economic challenges. The ultimate reason for this is the relative weakness of the state and the perceived lack of legitimacy of the regime or government in control. In the Middle East, this is ultimately due to the process of state formation and the subsequent artificiality of most of the borders of the region, including those of major oil-producing states such as Iraq, the Gulf states and

Libya, and the strength of supra-national ideologies, such as pan-Islamism or pan-Arabism (Anderson 1987; Schwartz 2008). The same complex and incomplete legacies of state formation are also evident in many other oil-exporting developing regions, such as Central Asia (Franke et al. 2009), Sub-Saharan Africa (Yates 1996; Soares de Oliveira 2007) and Latin America (Karl 1997).

The consequence is that the regimes in power in such oil-rich states have an overwhelming priority to maintain and secure their power. The possession of large oil deposits does not mean, as some of the resource curse literature suggests, that such governments are somehow autonomous from their societies – in reality, they are acutely aware that society has clear expectations that they should benefit from the abundance of these resources (Okruhlik 1999). In fact, it is the acuteness of the awareness of these expectations, and the narrow legitimacy of their rule, that generates a deep sense of insecurity among the regime elites. The result is an overwhelming focus on ensuring the short-term resilience of the regime rather than the longer-term development of the country. This requires attention on rewarding loyalty which, in a rentier state, is a question of the allocation of oil rents to the key clients who protect the regime, ensuring that this is also sufficiently widely dispersed that key popular constituencies also benefit. It also means that attention is given to ensuring effective security forces so as to be able to repress any dissent or any challenges to the distribution of power in the country. The consequence of this is a swollen military and security budget which further drains away resources from more focused developmental goals.

Resource-rich countries in the Middle East, as well as in other parts of the developing world, tend as a consequence to have strong patron–client (neo-patrimonial) and military (praetorian) characteristics. This is the main underlying reason for the prevalence of the resource curse, understood as the failure of resource-abundant states to diversify their economies in a sustainable and dynamic manner. However, it is important not to exaggerate the extent of this 'resource curse'. The original resource curse theory focused particularly on the period from 1970 to 1990 which was when oil price volatility was highest and a period of windfall profits ended with dramatic and unprecedented falls, leading to high levels of indebtedness (Sachs and Warner 1995; Humphreys et al. 2007). It was not surprising that the newly resource-rich states found it difficult to manage this particular experience. When different and longer time-sets are included, such as from 1980 to 2000, there is no clear evidence that resource-abundant countries have underperformed relative to other countries (Maloney 2002; Alexeev and Conrad 2009). There is similarly a question mark over whether resource-rich countries are inherently more authoritarian and repressive. As Haber and Menaldo have identified, the effect for most countries becoming resource producers has generally been politically neutral in the sense that the countries were authoritarian before the resource booms and remained so afterwards (Haber and Menaldo 2011). This is the case, for example, for the resource-rich countries in the Middle East and in the former Soviet Union. In both regions, authoritarianism is the historical norm rather than a resource-dependent anomaly.

However, these qualifications should not detract from recognizing the important insights provided by the literature on the rentier state and the resource curse. These include first the reality that the majority of resource-rich developing countries have failed to diversify their economies from dependence on the resource sector to generate broader sustainable economic growth. Developmental successes are in much shorter supply than those cases where economic performance has been distinctly disappointing. Second, resource-abundant developing countries have a strong tendency towards neo-patrimonial and praetorian regimes, where the resource rents available to these regimes, and the narrowly based elites that constitute these regimes, have helped to consolidate their power and longevity. Third, dependence on external resource rents generates significant domestic insecurities, whether these be high levels of societal insecurity, due to the repressive acts of the state, or regime insecurity leading to dysfunctional behaviour, ranging from isolationism to external aggression.

As has been argued previously, the fact of possession of substantial resources, such as oil, does not in itself explain the nature and content of these internal domestic insecurities. The broader historical context and legacies, and the complex regional and international dynamics, need to be incorporated to provide the overarching context. Nevertheless, it is the case that the specific nature of these domestic insecurities, and how states and societies seek to manage or challenge them, cannot be understood without including the political economy of the natural resource sectors. As the central theme of this book argues, it is the struggle for power, justice and legitimacy over the distribution of the resource wealth, rather than the resource itself, which is the principal causal mechanism for the insecurities generated.

Resource Wars

The argument so far is that there is an important distinction between those resource-rich states that have, and those that have not, successfully managed to utilize their natural resources to support industrialization, economic diversification and a sustainable economy. The difference is what has been presented in this chapter as the distinction between the resource blessing and the resource curse. The key argument is that the difference between these two conditions is not due to the physical nature of the resources themselves but to the socio-economic and political practices and institutions which either foster such economic policies or hinder and constrain them. In the former case, the state tends to be strong, cohesive and autonomous; in the latter case, the state has features of the rentier state with neo-patrimonial and praetorian structures and processes.

A further key research question is whether these oil-rich states, particularly those with strong neo-patrimonial and praetorian features, are particularly prone to violent conflict and civil wars. There has been a large and inconclusive academic debate with some differing results. For example, as noted above, Smith argued against the conflict-proneness assumption by noting that, for the period 1974–99, oil wealth is actually robustly associated with increased regime stability, even when controlling for repression, and with a lower likelihood of civil war (Smith 2004). Significantly, he found that neither boom nor bust periods exerted any particular effect on regime stability. However, other analysts have argued that oil exports are significantly correlated with civil war (de Soysa 2002; Fearon and Laitin 2002) and, in particular, with secessionist civil wars (Collier and Hoeffler 2002; Collier et al. 2003). Ross highlights how oil production leads to a higher risk of civil war conflict by comparing between oil and non-oil states, calculating that countries without petroleum faced a 2.8 per cent chance that a new conflict would break out; countries with petroleum had a 3.9 per cent chance, almost 40 per cent higher (Ross 2012). However, as Ross himself recognizes, civil wars are relatively rare events and the majority of oil-rich states 'have been conflict free' (Ross 2012: 154). Smith notes that rentier state and resource curse theorists tend to focus on the 'favourite cases' of Iran, Nigeria, Algeria and Venezuela, rather than the long-surviving Gulf Arab monarchs (Smith 2004: 240).

One way to think through this mixed evidence is to recognize that violence and insecurity, at differing levels and degrees, are a reality for citizens of authoritarian, neo-patrimonial and praetorian oil-abundant rentier states. These states might appear to be outwardly stable but they have a fundamental fragility in terms of their legitimacy given the narrow base of their structures of power and the lack of popular forms of political representation. Oil wealth provides a means and capacity to compensate for this legitimacy deficit, particularly if the resource wealth is abundant relative to the size of the population. For example, in the Gulf states, the indigenous population (if not all the foreign workers) have a clear material stake in the allocative functions of the state. Legitimation can also be generated through well-resourced ideological commitments, whether these be theocratic, as in Saudi Arabia or Iran, or secular nationalist, as in Iraq or Algeria. But all these states can never trust the efficacy of such positive inducements and ultimately rely on large and extensive internal security services to ensure that political protest is swiftly repressed. These states are, to use Michael Mann's typology, 'despotic' states whose power is ultimately based on the exemplary displays of violence rather than 'infrastructural' states capable of working synergistically through and with society (Mann 1993).

There is, therefore, an intrinsic fragility to the typical oil-rich rentier state. Stability can certainly be preserved for long periods through a careful balance of co-option and repression. The power given to elites in resource-rich countries to distribute oil rents certainly helps this process. The stability comes through a general acquiescence among elites and the broader population that the political order is either preferable to preserve or is too strong to be challenged. However, if the internal political order appears to be breaking down or has lost its central cohesion, then the condition of stability quickly shifts to instability and disorder. This happens, for example, when the political leadership changes and the structures of patronage and clientelism are no longer guaranteed and there is, therefore, great uncertainty about the new distribution of power and influence. In cases such as these, all the sublimated violence and longstanding grievances of differing groups can potentially surface and lead to civil conflict.

Recent examples of this can be seen in the regime transitions in Iraq in 2003 and in Libya in 2011. Both countries are archetypical examples of oil-rich rentier states which rely on a careful mix of co-option and political repression to preserve an authoritarian, neo-patrimonial and praetorian regime. Both regimes demonstrated considerable internal stability. Saddam Hussein and Muammar Gaddafi came to power at a period of considerable political flux in the Middle East and, benefiting from the oil booms of the 1970s, constructed highly personalized but durable and stable regimes which lasted over 30 years (Vandewalle 2006; Tripp 2007). Both leaders originated from minority groups and consolidated their power through relying on the loyalty of family and tribe, the co-option of other social groups and severe repression (for the case of Iraq, see Makiya 1998). Both regimes felt sufficiently internally secure to challenge the West through an activist and aggressive external policy, with Gaddafi seeking to extend his power in Central Africa and Hussein in the Gulf region. Both regimes were perceived to be supporting terrorism and to be engaged in chemical, biological and nuclear weapons proliferation. Both regimes also survived years of Western sanctions imposed upon them.

Ultimately, it was only full-scale Western military intervention that finally changed the political dispensation and ensured regime change. But, contrary to Western expectations, the result was not a shift towards a more pluralistic and inclusive society but a bitter and violent conflict which mixed longstanding historical grievances with a struggle over control of the distribution of the oil revenues. Since 2003, Iraq has become divided between its three main ethnic and confessional groups, the Kurds, Sunnis and Shi'a, with the Sunni population, which previously had political domination, feeling disenfranchised and willing to support violent secessionist and terrorist groups such as Islamic State (Dodge 2014). Since 2011, Libya has descended into virtual anarchy with two different contending governments, representing the west and the east of the country, and neither being capable of suppressing the multiple autonomous militias controlling different parts of the country (Cole and McQuinn 2015). These negative consequences of intervention illustrate well Mancur Olson's important point that it is generally better to have a 'stationary bandit', even if highly repressive, than to have a number of 'roving bandits' (Olson 1993). Iraq and Libya have essentially turned into 'failed states' through the disintegration of formerly internally stable, if deeply repressive, neo-patrimonial and praetorian states.

In both these cases, it is not oil in itself which is the cause of violent civil conflict. It is the perceived illegitimacy, combined with the capacity of social groups effectively to challenge the distributive networks of social and political power that control the allocation of the oil rents, which is critical. These conflicts are, as the central argument of the book contends, primarily a political struggle over the legitimacy and justice of existing power relations. These power struggles cannot be understood, however, without the decisive role that oil plays, not least in providing the key material resources that underpin the power and authority of central government.

When extrapolating more generally to resource-fuelled civil wars, there is undoubtedly an important dimension of these conflicts that is about the political economy and the material motivations or the 'greed' of the actors concerned (Collier and Hoeffler 2004). However, these material motivations are always inextricably linked to underlying ideological and political grievances (Ballentine and Sherman 2003). In oil-rich countries, these grievances often have a regional expression.

The enclave nature of oil, the fact that it is a 'point' resource generally concentrated in certain regions rather than diffused throughout the country, means that the most common civil conflict tends to pit central authority against peripheral regions (Le Billon 2001). This can be seen in a number of the most serious and longstanding oil and gas-linked civil wars. In Indonesia, the Aceh Freedom Movement challenged the central government for exploiting Aceh's natural gas and oil resources and fought for independence on the basis that, with secession from Indonesia, Aceh would be as rich as Brunei. The civil war continued from 1976 until 2005 when a new agreement, providing Aceh with 70 per cent of the oil and gas of the region, finally brought a peaceful settlement to the conflict (Renner 2015). Such a settlement has not been achieved in the Niger Delta, where there has been a constant struggle to gain greater regional control over the extensive oil and gas resources ever since the decision of the Nigerian government to treat oil as a centralized asset. After the repression of the Biafran secessionist war in the 1970s, the Niger Delta has remained poor while also suffering severe environmental degradation, leading to the formation of militant groups such as the Movement for the Emancipation of the Niger Delta (Watts 2004; Soares de Oliveira 2007). Similarly, it was the decision of the government in North Sudan to claim control over the oil fields in South Sudan which was central to the many years of civil war between the north and the south.

These cases demonstrate that the civil conflicts involving oil and other energy resources generally occur when the government fails to legitimate and justify the distribution and allocation of the revenues from these resources, and when there are also social groups or movements that are capable of and committed to violent resistance. In countries where such violent conflicts are endemic, the state can be said to have 'failed' in that it fails to fulfil its fundamental duty to provide security for its citizens. However, it is important to recognize that the wider population of resource-rich countries, which might appear outwardly stable, often include substantial domestic insecurities and structured relations of violence. Indeed, it is the nature of the rentier state, with its neo-patrimonial and praetorian features, to incorporate a significant set of repressive internal security institutions and practices.

Conclusion

The aim of the chapter has been to examine how domestic insecurities within energy-abundant countries contribute to energy insecurity. The main conclusion is that the impact is mixed. In many resource-rich countries, the domestic insecurities are successfully managed as the distribution and allocation of the revenues do not cause significant distributional conflicts and society generally benefits from the contribution of the sector to other parts of the economy. These countries can be said to have a resource blessing. There are, though, other states where the distributional outcomes remain deeply contested as the benefits are captured by a narrower segment of society and the resource wealth does not generate growth for other parts of the economy. It is to these oil-rich states that have failed to achieve their potential that the concept of the rentier state and its corollary, the resource curse theory, applies. There are also, though, those states where the resource curse has become so intense that the distributional conflicts have led to the failure of the state to maintain internal stability and there is violent civil conflict.

The principal argument of this chapter is that there is a strong linkage between state formation and the domestic insecurities generated by resource wealth. This has led to identifying three categories of resource-abundant state: the developed and developing; the neo-patrimonial and praetorian; and the failed or failing state. These different forms of states are then linked to differing general characteristics of resource-linked domestic security and insecurity, as summarized in table 5.1. However, it is important to stress that these categories represent what Max Weber calls 'ideal-types', and any particular state will inevitably fail to fall neatly into any of these categories without

Table 5.1   State Formation, the Resource Curse and Security

State Form of Resource-Rich State	State-Society Relations	Resource Blessing or Curse	Domestic Security
Strong state	Synergistic and pluralistic	Resource blessing	Secure
Weak state	Neo-patrimonial; praetorian	Resource curse	Insecure; repression and authoritarianism
Failed state	Disintegration; civil conflict	Resource wars	Extremely insecure: war and conflict

qualification, and the reality is generally messier and less clear. For example, resource-rich developed countries continue to be threatened by regional secessionism, as can be seen in Britain with the Scottish demand to take control of 'their oil'. As noted earlier, it is also difficult in practice to make a neat and easy distinction between 'developmental' and 'neo-patrimonial' developing states or clearly to identify the causal factors that lead to these different outcomes of state formation. The category of neo-patrimonial and praetorian also includes significant variation, as can be seen in the way that they are divided into pro-Western and anti-Western camps.

It is also important to emphasize that states in these three different categories are not isolated or disconnected from each other. The reality is a complex web of links and connections. Classical rentier states, such as the Gulf states, have close and intense relations with the West, whether with Western banks or companies or with Western militaries who guarantee their security. The elites of resource-rich countries, wherever they might be from, have their funds and often extensive properties in the West. When considering the high levels of indebtedness that the 'resource curse' led to in many resource-rich countries, it is also important to remember that some responsibility is due also to the Western banks and states that encouraged such counter-cyclical borrowing. The reality is that state-to-state interaction is only a relatively small part of the global energy market: there are a multiplicity of other powerful actors, particularly those which work within the global transnational economy. How this transnational market provides for, or threatens, energy security is the topic of the next chapter.

— 6 —
Energy Security and Energy Markets

In the theoretical and analytical framework for this book, a distinction was made between energy security as driven by deliberate and intentional political actions and those that are more indirect, complex and often unintentional. The analysis so far has focused primarily on the domain of intentional politically driven challenges and how different states have responded to these. With this political focus, the greater part of the analysis has been given to the international and domestic politics of oil and gas. This chapter shifts focus away from the political to the economic, examining the more diverse and complex interactions of energy markets and how these raise significant but often inadvertent energy security challenges. This chapter addresses the broader political economy question of the relationship between states and markets and how this is contested and challenged in the energy sector. Both states and markets have a common interest in ensuring economic growth through the efficient operation of energy markets; states have, though, broader responsibilities to ensure that such markets support the security of their citizens as well as meet societal expectations of sustainability and justice. States and energy markets cannot therefore be neatly separated; they are in constant tension and renegotiation of their respective spheres of operation which is an inextricably political process.

This chapter breaks this complex and potentially abstract issue down to a more concrete basis through examination of the different markets and distinctive political economies of the most important global energy fuels and flows – coal, oil, nuclear, gas and renewables. For each of these energy markets, the key overarching question is the relationship between energy security and economic efficiency or competitiveness. In practice, it is not possible to isolate these two dimensions and treat them as a binary choice; there are other factors, social, political and increasingly environmental, which need to be included in the analysis. Going back to the core argument of the book, this chapter focuses primarily on the tensions and trade-offs between the values of security and prosperity, while recognizing that other values, such as sustainability and political justice, are inherently part of the analysis.

In terms of its structure, this chapter follows a quasi-historical trajectory in that it deals with energy resources in the broad order that they emerged historically as inputs into modernization and development. This chapter can be seen as a companion to chapter 3 which dealt with the history of energy security. The story starts with coal which fuelled the first industrial revolutions from the nineteenth century onwards; it then moves to oil which assumed growing importance with fast growth in the post-World War II period; to nuclear which offered the promise, if not ultimately the realization, of a transformation in energy supply from the 1950s onwards; to natural gas which has increasingly come to assume that promise of the future which nuclear originally offered; and finally to modern renewables which now have arguably the greatest weight of global expectations for a transition to a sustainable energy system.

While the ordering logic is historically rooted, the focus of the analysis is contemporary and relates to current conditions and dynamics. What emerges from the analysis is that the tendency to present the development of the energy sector in a linear sequential trajectory only captures a part of the picture. Certainly, the initial coal-dominated industrial systems, the 'Coal Age', were increasingly supplanted by the oil-based systems, the 'Oil Age', and that a shift is now evident towards developing the primacy of electricity-based systems, the 'Elektron Age' (Bressand 2013: 22–3). But it is important to qualify this picture by noting that the dynamic is as much cumulative as sequential. As new energy sources have been introduced, such as nuclear, natural gas and modern renewables, traditional fuels, such as coal and oil, have not disappeared or been displaced. They have succeeded in maintaining significant shares of global energy markets (see figure 3.1). Indeed, it was coal, the oldest of the modern fuels, that actually enjoyed the greatest growth in demand in the first decade of the twenty-first century.

It is a key argument of this chapter that this development of a globally diverse fuel mix is driven significantly by energy security concerns. States and companies have generally been more cautious and incremental than radical and transformative. The reasons for this conservative approach include a mix of powerful producer interests and lobbies, institutional and technological barriers, and broader social preferences. But there is also the preference of states, confronted by more complex energy systems and conflicting and often irreconcilable societal interests, to opt for diversity, for not 'putting all your eggs in one basket', as a deliberate strategy for ensuring energy security (Stirling 2010). Whether this approach is adequate to meet the environmental challenges of the future, most notably in relation to climate change, is the subject of the next chapter. This chapter focuses its analysis on energy fuels and sources as they are used in practice, starting with the seeming paradox of the survival of what many consider to be the dirty relic of the nineteenth century – coal.

The Great Survivor: Coal

The continuing importance of coal in global energy markets, taking 29 per cent of global market share in 2014, appears a historical anomaly (figure 6.1; Tyfield 2014: 60). The fact that coal remains the dirtiest of the main fossil fuels adds to this sense of historical anachronism with coal responsible for 44 per cent of global carbon dioxide emissions and over half of air pollution in many countries (Martin 2015: 5). The high levels of pollution and smog that regularly affect Chinese cities are directly linked to the high levels of coal used in the country. Western countries have managed to clean up most of their cities, avoiding the types of coal-induced smog that in London in 1952 caused over 5,000 deaths. However, the pollution caused by the continuing dependence on coal-fired power plants is still very considerable with, for example, US coal power resulting in an estimated '115 million tons of ash, sludge and airborne effluents, much of it bearing the

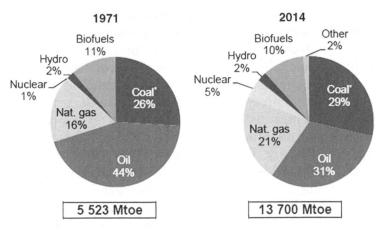

* Peat and oil shale are aggregated with coal

Figure 6.1   Total Primary Energy Supply by Fuel, 1971 and 2014
Source: © OECD/IEA 2016 Key World Energy Trends (Excerpt from world energy balances), IEA Publishing. Licence www.iea.org/t&c

noxious tidings of mercury, cadmium, lead, arsenic and even radiation' (Montgomery 2010: 127).

There is, though, an alternative vision of the role of coal in contemporary global energy markets. This is in its contribution to the process of electrification which brings many of the benefits of modern civilization – cheap and clean lighting, heating, cooking, refrigeration and other labour-saving devices (Hughes 1983; Nye 2010). Coal's role has, over time, been increasingly concentrated in this sector with 85 per cent of the fuel being employed as 'steam coal' for electricity. Currently, the demand for this has come most strongly from developing countries in the process of economic development and industrialization. Coal has, for example, been the principal fuel behind the rapid economic development in China. China's coal consumption almost tripled from the early 2000s and, by 2015, the country alone accounted for half of global coal demand. Given that coal has accounted for 70–80 per cent of China's total primary energy supply over the past three decades, the Chinese economic miracle cannot be divorced from its fundamental dependence on cheap and plentiful supplies of coal (Cornot-Gandolphe 2014: 6–7). Until very recently, the environmental costs of this have been viewed as a necessary side-effect of the multiple benefits that have come from fast economic growth, including electrification and industrialization (Andrews-Speed and Dannreuther 2011: 43–4). Other developing countries, such as India, Bangladesh and Indonesia, are increasingly making the same calculation that coal is an inextricable and necessary part of their broader development strategy, despite the prospective environmental damage caused (Smil 2010: 69). Figure 6.2 illustrates not only the very large growth in demand for coal but also how its share of the Asian energy fuel mix has increased significantly since the 1970s.

Coal has, in reality, a number of advantages compared to other fossil fuels. The first is the geographical distribution of global supplies of coal. Unlike oil and gas, coal is more equitably distributed across the world. This is most

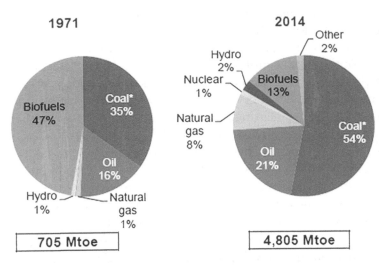

1971   2014

705 Mtoe   4,805 Mtoe

* Peat and oil shale are aggregated with coal

Figure 6.2 Total Primary Energy Supply, Asia, 1971 and 2014
Source: © OECD/IEA 2016 Key World Energy Trends
(Excerpt from world energy balances), IEA Publishing. Licence
www.iea.org/t&c

evident in the Asia-Pacific region, which enjoys only 3 per
cent of global oil and gas reserves but has relatively abundant coal supplies. The global ranking of countries by
reserves includes major Asian as well as Western states:
United States (27%), Russia (17%), China (13%), India
(10%), Australia (9%), Germany (7%) and South Africa
(5%). In energy security terms, coal's most significant
benefit is that it provides critical protection for a number
of major powers from dependence on oil supplies from the
Persian Gulf region. Indeed, coal enjoyed a major renaissance in the West in response to the 1970s oil crisis when
most Western countries diversified away from oil in power
generation and reverted back, at least in part, to the use
of coal in the generation of electricity (Landsberg 1987;
Camp 2014). Unlike other fossil fuels, most of the coal
supplies are used domestically with only 15 per cent traded
internationally, with the US, Russia, Australia and Indonesia being the major exporting producers. There are also

abundant reserves of coal with an estimated 861 billion tonnes of proven coal reserves worldwide, which translates into enough coal to last around 112 years at current rates of production. In contrast, proven oil and gas reserves are equivalent to around 46–54 years at current production levels. There is, as a consequence, much less of a 'peak coal' than a 'peak oil' debate, and there is confidence that coal remains the most abundant of the remaining fossil fuels (Ericsson and Soderholm 2013: 227).

Apart from its more even geographical distribution, the relative cheapness and economic competitiveness of coal is the second major factor which ensures the continuing demand for coal. As of 2016, the price of coal had dropped to $40 per tonne which makes it competitive with gas and oil in most parts of the world. The international market for coal does not have the same price volatility as with oil and gas. It is this combination of relative geographical abundance and cheapness which makes coal the energy security fuel of choice. Coal also has a significant advantage that, unlike gas, biomass or electricity, it is relatively cheap and easy to store which means that governments, utilities and power plants can easily stockpile the fuel as a hedge against future supply disruptions or price increases.

For developing countries with urgent social, economic and political demands for fast economic growth, it is not surprising that domestically produced and relatively cheap and secure supplies of coal are exploited to provide the preferred energy pathway towards modernity. After China and India, the next waves of coal exploitation for purposes of fast development are likely to come from Vietnam, Bangladesh, Indonesia and Cambodia, which all have large populations and significant coal industries. But even in the developed Western countries on a post-industrial trajectory, the benefits and attraction of coal for power generation remain powerful. In the electricity sector, there is significant competition between coal and gas. Gas is significantly cleaner and more efficient than coal; however, particularly in liberalized electricity markets, coal is still legitimately chosen on cost grounds. For example, when gas prices increased significantly in Europe during the 2000s, there was a resurgence in commissioning of coal-fired power stations (Hamm and Borison 2008; Pahle 2010).

One of the European countries where the recent 'dash to coal' is intuitively surprising is Germany, given the strong societal commitments towards renewables and the mitigation of climate change. As Pahle (2010) notes, there are many factors behind the decision to invest substantially in new coal power plants which go beyond strictly cost considerations. However, a key element is that, in Germany, as in other coal-producing countries, there is a sizeable domestic workforce and thus political constituency in support of coal. As was discussed in chapter 3, coal mining communities have historically played a leading and often highly militant role in national politics (Church et al. 1991; Mitchell 2011: 18–31). In the final analysis, there remains significant political pressure in Germany, as in other countries with substantial mining communities, to avoid large job losses in the industry. In domestic political terms in Europe, it is easier to disappoint gas suppliers as they are primarily foreigners and thus without an electoral vote. Poland has similarly sought to defend its large coal production through highlighting the energy security gains for Europe of a reduction of dependence on Russian gas, despite the environmental costs of continued coal use. In the United States, the traditionally militant coal-mining communities have lost much of their power but the coal industry as a whole maintains a powerful voice, particularly in the Republican Party, through opposing clean air and anti-pollution legislation and by questioning the scientific credibility of human-induced climate change. This power was evident in the victory of Donald Trump in the 2016 US elections where defence of coal mining was a central plank of his campaign.

A final significant factor which promotes coal's continued use and seeks to mitigate its negative environmental image is the promise of 'clean coal' (Fitzgerald 2012). This concept offers the prospect of a 'near zero-emissions' coal power plant, something that the US FutureGen project proclaimed as its goal when initiated in 2003. However, as Montgomery notes, the more accurate claim would be 'cleaner' rather than 'clean coal' as the targeted capabilities would greatly reduce, but not eliminate, pollutants. The end effect would be to make coal use equivalent to the cleanliness of natural gas, a significant improvement but not without environmental harms (Montgomery 2010: 106). There are also a number of challenges to establishing and installing a clean coal technological system. These include treating or washing coal before use to reduce toxic impurities; gasifying coal before combustion, utilizing the much more efficient integrated gasification combined cycle (IGCC); and then ensuring capture of the carbon and its long-term storage. All of this adds significantly to operational costs. IGCC is about 20–25 per cent more expensive than conventional pulverized coal plants; carbon capture and storage (CCS) adds between 39 and 64 per cent to the costs of the electricity produced (Watson and Jones 2015: 230). This makes the role of government support vital, particularly in developing CCS. However, the record is not good, with only one carbon capture system in commercial operation in 2015 at a power station, the Boundary Dam coal plant in Canada (Clark 2015). Multiple other power plant CCS ventures have been scrapped and mothballed, including the much vaunted FutureGen project, which lost its federal funding in 2012. The CCS projects that have been most successful have been those that have used the carbon for enhanced oil recovery in regions, such as in Canada, with significant depleted oil fields. This has further eroded the environmental credentials of CCS.

According to the IEA, to ensure a sustainable global energy system which limits average temperature increases to 2 per cent would require CCS to be fitted to 32 per cent of all coal-fired power plant capacity by 2035 (IEA 2016). This illustrates both the expectation that coal will continue to have strong demand in the medium term and that mitigation of its effects will require very substantial progress in terms of carbon capture and storage. As noted above, the immediate signs for such widespread take-up of CCS are not encouraging. Nevertheless, there are indications that coal might finally be facing significant pressures as a consequence of environmental constraints. The UK is the first developed country to indicate that it intends to decommission and not replace its coal power stations; in the US, the mix of more rigorous federal clean power regulations along with abundant supplies of relatively cheap gas is leading to a phasing out of coal-fired power stations. The Chinese government has also stated clearly that it intends to reduce the contribution of coal in its energy mix and combat air pollution and climate change (Mathews and Tan 2015). While coal consumption will be capped, particularly in the Eastern provinces of China, coal is likely to continue to play a dominant role, with increases in production and use in the poorer Western provinces, so the overall impact of this policy remains ambiguous (Cornot-Gandolphe 2014: 11–12). Overall, there are many challenges ahead in making global progress in mitigating the environmental damage caused by coal to offset its clear economic and energy security advantages.

Fading Dominance: Oil?

Oil, to a significantly greater extent than coal, defines the contemporary modern world. Crude oil's comparative advantage is its high energy density and its transportability. It produces an array of fuels, lubricants, waxes, greases and tars, which has made possible the spread of the internal combustion engine into every conceivable form of transportation. Oil is the fuel used in 95 per cent of the world's transportation, providing the crucial ingredient for modern mobile society. Oil is also superior to coal in other sectors such as power generation, industry and commercial and residential heating. Its practical advantages include its capacity to burn hotter, to produce more power and less smoke, and to be easier to store and transport. Oil also produces a huge variety of products which are pervasive in modern living, such as plastics, drugs, fertilizers, cosmetics and paints.

The puzzle is not why oil remains a fuel in demand but rather why its dominance is not greater. A number of the reasons for this have already been addressed in the historical sections of this book. Oil's period of greatest dominance was in the 1950s and 1960s when oil powered the economic recovery of the industrialized world after World War II. The energy security shocks of the 1970s radically undermined global confidence and heightened anxieties about the reliability and affordability of future supplies of oil. The result was a concerted drive to find substitutes for oil, the most significant of these being in power generation and space heating where, as noted above, coal found an unexpected renewed demand and natural gas rapidly gained market share. Oil was essentially eliminated in the developed world from the power generation mix except in niche sectors such as stand-by generation capacity.

Although oil has continued to dominate the transportation sector, it is important to note that this is not inevitable. Half of Brazil's petrol consumption comes from biofuels and the US and Europe similarly include plant-based fuels for their transportation needs. It should also be noted that other fossil fuels, such as coal and gas, can be converted into liquids for the transport sector, though there are substantial capital and environmental costs. There is also the possibility of substitution through transformation, especially through the use of electricity to make substantial inroads into the transportation sector, through the expansion of hybrid and electric cars. Thus, while oil remains a special fuel, with substantial comparative advantages in terms of energy density and transportability, it is theoretically substitutable and, politically, there are strong pressures to move in this direction.

There are a number of ways in which the specific features of the global oil market contribute to this desire to move away from dependence on oil. The first is in the ways that states, rather than markets, play a major role in directing the industry, particularly in how such state intervention contributes to the phenomenon of resource nationalism. As highlighted in previous chapters, a major source of energy insecurity is the perception that resource-producing countries use their access to vital energy supplies to gain economic and political advantage over the consuming states (Bremmer 2009; Vivoda 2009).

The extent to which this is a real problem or danger needs to be put into perspective. One of the impacts of the oil crisis in the 1970s was to break up the vertical integration of the industry, which had previously been dominated by the large international oil companies. The consequence of this was that the downstream refining and retail outlets in importing countries were broken apart, significantly increasing the fungibility of crude oil and progressively liberalizing the international oil market. Over time this led to the creation of oil futures contracts and spot oil markets in New York and London. The economic and political consequences of this significantly limited the prospective power of the oil-producing OPEC states and their newly nationalized oil companies. With oil now flowing freely on the global markets, it became impossible for individual or groups of oil-producing states to impose an oil embargo. In addition, OPEC never managed to match the previous cartel power of the Western oil companies, the so-called 'Seven Sisters', and consistently failed to steer oil production and thus control prices. Interventions to seek to manipulate oil prices were generally inefficient and often counter-productive, with prices more strongly driven by the market fundamentals of demand and supply (Goldthau and Witte 2009a: 375–7).

However, in one critical area, the resource nationalist sovereign powers of the oil-producing states have increased and this is in the upstream sector. In contrast to the 1960s when almost all of the world's oil reserves were controlled by international oil companies (IOCs), by the 1980s over 80 per cent of the world's global oil reserves were controlled by national oil companies (NOCs) (Marcel 2006; Chen and Jaffe 2007; Stevens 2008). Many large oil-rich states, such as Saudi Arabia and Mexico, have made their territory strictly off-limits to foreign investment. From a global perspective, the consequence is that there is no well-functioning multilateral market-centric investment regime whereby investment flows to the most efficient and profitable locations. In fact, the opposite is often the case as investment is made to produce oil in conditions, such as deep offshore, which are many times more expensive than the oil which could be exploited in the Persian Gulf region.

It is this peculiarity of the oil market that is the reason why rent is such a powerful and pervasive force in the industry. With low-cost producers limiting the amount they produce, higher-cost producers act as marginal suppliers to the industry. The excessive profits that are then generated are either captured by the low-cost producers through rents appropriated by the state or by the importing consuming states who impose significant petroleum taxes. In many developed countries, the substantial subsidies that exist for other energy sources, such as renewables or nuclear or even coal, are in effect made fiscally neutral by the substantial taxation on petroleum products. In many developing states, the temptation is the reverse of this, with governments directly subsidizing their citizens to reduce the costs of fossil fuels or, as in oil-producing states, using indirect subsidies to charge the non-market 'real extraction cost' of the oil, despite the negative impacts on the revenues of their NOCs. Overall, this means that the allocation of resources into this sector in both exporting and consuming countries is far from what would be the case if a free market were operating.

The particularities of the global oil market generate significant international tensions and suspicions. Consuming states tend to view oil-producing states as rapacious and politically ambitious, seeking to maximize economic rents and failing to invest sufficiently for future demand. Oil-exporting states, in turn, tend to see the major Western consuming states as promoting 'demand destruction' and deliberately undermining their economic future through policy mandates, taxation and subsidization of alternative fuels. All of this is exacerbated by the volatility of oil prices and the lack of regional and global energy institutions and regimes which might support greater transparency and the more effective operation of the market. The IEA and OPEC are the leading international bodies in the oil sector but they reflect the particular interests of the developed consuming states and the producing states respectively (Van de Graaf 2012). The International Energy Forum, which tries to bring the interests of the two sides together, remains a much weaker institution.

Despite all these insecurities and market imperfections, it is premature to assert that oil's future is inevitably one of decline. The economic security and prosperity of modern societies is deeply intertwined with oil use and the technological lock-in of the contemporary oil-fired civilization is deeply entrenched. No other fuel has the same advantages as oil in terms of energy density and transportability. There are also ways that market conditions can shift to strengthen the future prospects for oil. This can be seen in the rapid decline in the cost of a barrel of oil from over $100 in the early 2010s to under $30 during 2016. Although this was primarily driven by shifts in the fundamentals of supply and demand, a significant element was the decision by Saudi Arabia to maintain its production, foregoing the maximization of revenues so as to protect market share. The principal target of this was on more expensive oil production, such as shale oil production in the US. More generally, the impact of low prices can also potentially mirror what occurred in the 1980s, when oil prices similarly dropped, and the efforts to improve energy efficiency and find substitutes for oil declined, resulting in demand for oil regaining its powerful dominant position.

The Unfulfilled Promise – Nuclear

There was a time in the 1950s and 1960s when oil was viewed as the transition fuel to a quasi-utopian nuclear-powered energy future. In his 'Atoms for Peace' speech in 1953, US President Eisenhower urged that nuclear materials should be used for peaceful purposes to 'provide abundant electrical energy in the power-starved world' (Herring 2007). A famous prediction of that period was that electrical energy would become 'too cheap to meter'. During the 1960s and 1970s, nuclear energy also provided a counter to anxieties over energy security as a consequence of increased dependence on oil from the Middle East. It similarly provided some protection against the militancy and regular strikes in domestic coal-mining industries.

A key comparative advantage of nuclear power is that it generates large amounts of energy from small amounts of fuel. While a kilogram of coal typically yields about 3 kWh of electricity, the same weight of nuclear fuel produces 400,000 kWh (Montgomery 2010: 133). Supplies of uranium ore are reasonably widely distributed geographically, are easy to store and there are limited concerns about the future availability of supplies. There are also a number of ways to maximize the energy potential of the uranium used, either through reprocessing or through use of breeder reactors which creates new fissionable material at the same time as it consumes the original fuel.

More recently, there has again been an expectation of a 'nuclear renaissance'. This is driven by the benefits that nuclear power offers to counter pollution and anthropogenic climate change (Rhodes and Beller 2000; Toke 2013). When nuclear power plants are operating, they yield zero emissions over their entire life span that can extend for 50–60 years and the performance of nuclear in terms of life-cycle emissions is better even than many modern renewables, such as solar photovoltaic (PV). While a typical fossil fuel power plant will produce thousands of tonnes of noxious gases, particulates and heavy-metal-bearing and radioactive ash, including solid hazardous waste, a 1,000-Mwe nuclear plant releases no noxious gases or other pollutants and will produce about 30 tonnes of high-level waste. Globally, nuclear power saves the atmosphere over 500 million tonnes of carbon each year. These clear advantages of nuclear power in terms of mitigating the dangers of uncontrolled carbon emissions have led to some leading environmentalists taking an increasingly positive attitude towards nuclear energy (Goldemberg et al. 1988; Sustainable Development Commission 2006; Srinivasan and Rethinaraj 2013).

Despite the potential energy security and climate benefits, nuclear power has generally failed to fulfil earlier optimistic projections. According to the World Nuclear Association, at the end of 2015 there were 439 reactors in thirty countries, with a combined installed capacity of 383 Gigawatt electric (Gwe). A further sixty-six are under construction, of which twenty-four are in China, eight in Russia, and six in India, though a number of these have been under construction for a long time. Overall, the share of nuclear in the energy mix and the total amount of nuclear electricity have declined over time. The share of nuclear in electricity generation has dropped from 17 per cent in 1993 to about 11 per cent in 2015, and nuclear represents only about a 5 per cent share of global primary energy production. Projections indicate that nuclear production will potentially grow by as much as 60 per cent from 2015 to 2035 but that other sources of generation would grow even more rapidly so that the overall share of nuclear in total generation will decline.

The countries that have taken the plunge and developed a substantial nuclear power industry have tended to do so for two main reasons – power and prestige, and energy security. It is perhaps not surprising that the countries that were at the forefront of developing nuclear weapons programmes have also developed significant civilian nuclear power programmes. The United States, Russia, the United

Kingdom and France have been at the forefront of the nuclear industry, reaffirming their status as great powers, and they were driven by a certain missionary zeal to demonstrate the positive benefits, as against the evident destructive capabilities, of the nuclear revolution (Gowing and Arnold 1974; Goldberg and Rosner 2011; Cox et al. 2016). It is not surprising, in this context, that the fast developing emerging countries, such as China and India, are similarly drawn to the allure of nuclear power as an attribute of great power status. Countries with a particularly acute sense of vulnerability in terms of energy security have also been attracted to nuclear power. These include countries like Japan, which is almost totally dependent on energy imports, and a number of countries in Scandinavia and Central and East European countries that similarly suffer from significant energy security concerns. France, which has combined both a great power ambition with significant energy security concerns, has been the most ambitious in its nuclear power programme, with over 75 per cent of its electricity generated from nuclear energy (Hecht 2009).

A common feature of all the countries that have successfully promoted a nuclear power programme is the activist role of the state and the dominance of a technocratic elite. Sovacool and Valentine (2010) illustrate this particular 'socio-political economy' through an examination of the evolution of nuclear energy in France. They note that the origins of this programme lay with a humiliated and defeated France embracing a technocratic model with a strong state involved in guiding economic development; the development of highly centralized national energy planning within which the nuclear power programme played a central role; the constant promotion and association of the nuclear programme with national reconstruction around high-tech industry; the dominant role played by technocratic ideology in policy decisions; and the subordination of challenges to political authority, including limiting civic activism, in the expansion of nuclear power.

The authors argue that similar catalysts or drivers can be seen to be in the development of nuclear power in India and China.

This statist and technocratic model does, though, have its vulnerabilities, particularly if things go wrong. Three major nuclear accidents, in particular, have occurred that have represented major challenges to the nuclear industry and have had strong impacts on the expansion and contraction of the industry (see figure 6.3). The Three Mile Island accident in the United States in 1979 brought to an end the first period of nuclear optimism, generating increased social activism and anxieties over nuclear safety. There were also concerns that nuclear technology was simply not compatible with democratic accountability and that secrecy and lack of transparency are inherent to nuclear institutions and decision-making (Hultman and Koomey 2013). A second resurgence in the industry in the early 1980s was brought to a halt with the Chernobyl accident in the Soviet Union in 1986, which remains the worst nuclear accident on record. This had a lasting impact on Germany, for instance, paving the way for the decision to phase out nuclear power in that country (Schreurs 2012). The latest 'nuclear renaissance' was similarly severely challenged by the Fukushima accident in Japan in

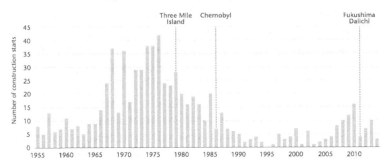

Figure 6.3   Nuclear Reactor Construction Starts, 1955–2014
Source: IAEA Power Reactor Information System (PRIS), available at: http://www.iaea.org/pris

2011, which was triggered by the effects of a tsunami and an earthquake. Although the damage caused by the accident was less extensive than feared, it resurrected concerns over nuclear safety and the capacity to deal with and plan for natural hazards and low-probability but high-risk scenarios (Elliot 2013; Rose and Sweeting 2016; Wheatley et al. 2016). The most worrying revelation was how there had developed, among the technocratic elites surrounding the nuclear industry in Japan, the so-called 'nuclear village', a dense network of corruption, collusion and nepotism that had led to the neglect of safety controls, the suppression of damaging information and a broader culture of self-censorship by the media and by professional and academic specialists (National Diet of Japan 2012; Tanter 2013: 475–6).

The prevalent lack of trust in the nuclear industry, and the concern over the power that it accrues to an unaccountable technocratic elite, is also exacerbated by the links between nuclear power and nuclear weapons. In theory, the two should be considered as distinct and separate categories, and the 1968 Nuclear Non-Proliferation Treaty (NPT) gives this concrete expression. The heart of the NPT is a grand bargain where non-nuclear weapons states have the right to the technology to develop civilian nuclear uses, while nuclear weapons are limited to the officially recognized nuclear weapons states who will be committed to nuclear disarmament. However, in practice, peaceful and military applications of nuclear technology cannot be clearly separated; uranium enrichment and plutonium separation can provide fissile material either for generating electricity or for explosive applications (Yudin 2013: 208). Despite safeguards within the NPT and its main formal body, the International Atomic Energy Agency (IAEA), a number of countries have exploited a civilian nuclear programme to develop nuclear weapons, whether through not being party to the NPT (India, Pakistan and Israel) or through not complying with the treaty (Iran and North Korea). The threat that the expansion of nuclear power might also contribute to horizontal nuclear proliferation sets an additional set of constraints against the global development of the industry (Dannreuther 2013: 240–5).

The final constraint against nuclear power is more mundane but potentially even more consequential. This is the economics of the industry. One of the aspects of the highly statist and technocratic evolution of the industry is that, as the *Economist* has noted, nuclear power is a 'creature of politics, not economics' (Economist 2012). While operational nuclear power plants produce electricity cheaply, the construction of such plants is expensive with very large up-front costs. In contrast with other electricity generation technologies, nuclear power has seen its construction costs increase over time, particularly with the need to enhance safety features (Boccard 2014). As a consequence, there have been growing construction delays and cost over-runs, particularly in the US and Europe, with, for example, the new nuclear plant in Normandy in France originally budgeted to cost €3bn and to be completed by 2012 but now estimated to be finished by 2018 at a cost of €10.5bn (Rangel and Leveque 2015). Major nuclear energy utilities have as a consequence seen their income decline and debts increase, particularly as such utilities also generally have to incorporate the costs of spent fuel management, waste disposal and decommissioning, which puts them at a disadvantage with fossil fuel power providers. The dilemma that states face is the extent to which subsidies for the industry are justifiable – a carbon tax is one which is seen as potentially equalizing the playing field. However, even in France, economic considerations are being taken more seriously, influencing the decision of the government of François Hollande to reduce the share of nuclear from over 70 to 50 per cent in the electricity sector (Schneider 2013). In liberalized energy markets, building nuclear power plants is essentially no longer a commercially feasible option. This is evident, for example, in the United States, where the decline in the cost of gas, mainly due to the shale gas revolution and increased US production, has tilted the balance decisively to natural gas-fired power generation.

The Rush to Gas?

The story of gas is almost the reverse of that of nuclear. In the past, gas was often unwanted and viewed as unprofitable and was routinely flared or just left in the ground. During the period 1970–90, the market share of gas in the global primary energy mix (once the Soviet Union is excluded) hardly changed, even though gas reserves increased significantly. The reasons for this included a sense of pessimism about future supplies, which contributed to the US and EU imposing restrictions and preventing gas from being used in industry and power generation. With the oil shocks in the 1970s, gas was thought also to pose energy security risks which meant that coal and nuclear tended to be privileged. As noted earlier, coal was the primary substitute for oil in the transformation of the power sector in the 1970s. It is ironic, when looked at retrospectively, that the Shah of Iran was recommended by Western advisers in the 1970s to develop nuclear power so as to preserve the country's oil and gas reserves for exports.

By the beginning of the new century, the image of gas had been transformed. It is now regularly viewed as a major expanding fuel for the future (IEA 2011). In contrast to the 1970s, the concerns over supplies have diminished and, in comparison with oil, conventional gas reserves are estimated to be relatively abundant and, in the absence of a truly global market, under-utilized. One measure of this is that of the 750 billion barrels of oil-equivalent that civilization has used by 2008, less than a quarter was from gas (Montgomery 2010: 89). With the new technology used in the US to exploit unconventional gas, global reserves are likely to go far higher.

Gas also has the advantage of versatility. It has a multiplicity of uses in industry, manufacturing, residential and commercial heating and, most importantly, in power generation. The development of the combined-cycle gas turbine power station (CCGT) in the 1970s represented a revolution in thermal efficiency, increasing the efficiency levels of a single-steam turbine power station from around 33 per cent to levels of 50 and even 60 per cent (Cragg 2013: 67). As a consequence, gas became the fuel of choice in the power sector. This comparative advantage has been further enhanced by the environmental advantages of gas. Gas is much less polluting than either oil or coal, yielding almost no sulphur dioxide or particulates and 30 per cent less CO_2 than oil and 50 per cent less than coal. In addition, gas is the best fuel to complement the growth of renewables, such as wind and solar, in power generation. Only gas turbines are sufficiently flexible in responding to and being able to fill the gaps that occur due to the fluctuations and intermittency of wind power and other renewable energy sources.

Gas has, as a consequence, become the new 'transition' fuel. It is a fuel that is seen to be best placed to make fast reductions in the global use of coal and thus be the critical catalyst for reduction in global carbon emissions. There is also a potential, though still in its infancy, for gas to displace oil in the transportation sector; this is a rapidly growing sector which is expected to reach 2.5 per cent of total gas use by 2018. Gas is also seen to play a critical role as the essential backing for the ambitious targets for increased power generation from renewables. Overall, the share of gas in the global primary energy mix is, therefore, set to increase over the next twenty years, from 24.4 per cent to 26.1 per cent in 2035 (BP 2014).

This projected expansion is not, though, of as great a magnitude as the potential advantages of switching to gas from other fossil fuels appear to suggest. This reflects the fact that there also exist significant constraints and limitations to the formation of a truly global gas market which would compete with oil and, in terms of price, with coal. The main problem is that gas is far less dense and energy-rich than liquid petroleum – for a given volume at standard pressure, it contains only a fraction of the heat content of oil. The consequence is that gas is far more difficult and more expensive to transport than oil. The only way that gas can be transported over land is by pipelines and this 'tyranny of distance' has meant that gas has a number of regional, rather than truly global, markets. While gas is a relatively cheap commodity, with no cartel like OPEC generating additional rents, the transportation costs are substantial and are a large part of the overall costs. Large gas projects are similar to expensive offshore oil projects in that they are capital-intensive and involve substantial up-front costs. Given the complexity and size of these projects, states are inevitably involved. The development of the gas pipeline network from the Soviet Union to Western Europe in the 1980s is paradigmatic of the intense state-to-state negotiation and cooperation required (Hog-selius 2013). Gas trade, in contrast to oil, generally requires long-term contracts if it is to be feasible, principally because of the capital-intensive projects and the need for long-term guarantees of supply and demand to make the trade worthwhile for both buyers and sellers.

The economic costs of developing gas trade is also exacerbated by perceptions of political risk. Gas is similar to oil in the ways that energy security concerns are pervasive and affect decision-making. In Europe, energy security concerns towards gas are arguably greater than those towards oil, with Russia being seen to use gas as a geopolitical weapon against its former Soviet neighbours, thereby undermining security of supply to the EU states (Bradshaw 2009: 1928–30). Transit states in the gas pipeline route are also particular sources of vulnerability as they have the power to disrupt flows of gas and have an incentive to bargain for improved terms (Stevens 2009). As with oil supplies, gas reserves are concentrated in a relatively small number of countries, with the greatest concentrations in

Iran (18%), Russia (16.8%) and Qatar (13.3%). As with oil, the Asia-Pacific region has very limited gas supplies; with the decline in North Sea gas, Europe is also becoming more dependent on imports.

Energy security concerns combined with the formidable difficulties of delivering gas to its customers has, therefore, limited the expansion of gas markets. These remain regionally fragmented with differing regional pricing mechanisms which are often indexed to the price of other commodities, such as oil, rather than spot prices linked to gas fundamentals. The consequence of this is that gas prices have often been relatively expensive compared to other fuels, such as coal, and have experienced considerable volatility. For example, from 2000 to 2008 gas prices increased considerably, mirroring the increase in oil prices, thus increasing the competitiveness of coal.

Two developments have, though, heralded the potential for a radical change in the structure of global gas production and trade. The first is driven by advances in liquefied natural gas (LNG) technology which has led to significant reductions in the cost of LNG projects. LNG technology is not new and Japan has been importing LNG gas in ever-increasing quantities since the 1970s. But, with the reduction in costs, other countries in the Asia-Pacific as well as in Europe and the US have been increasing their share. The advantage of LNG is that it can reach markets which are otherwise inaccessible by pipeline and can also provide markets for what would otherwise be 'stranded gas' (Van Groenendaal 1999). LNG supply also helps to mitigate energy security concerns by potentially offering gas-importing countries additional suppliers and reducing the dependence on pipeline gas suppliers. This has helped both China and the EU in its ambition to reduce dependence on Russia (Hulbert and Goldthau 2013: 105–6). The growth of the LNG market has also offered the prospect of the integration of the hitherto regional markets and that, like oil in the 1970s, there could emerge an efficient market with a global gas price (Massachusetts Institute of

Technology 2010). If this were to occur, this would facilitate the expansion of a global gas market.

The second development is the more unexpected emergence of unconventional gas on a huge scale in the United States. US shale gas production has grown from 6 billion cubic feet in 2007 to 27 billion cubic feet in 2014, with the US overtaking Russia as the largest gas producer in the world. By 2040, it is projected that shale gas will represent half of US gas production. The impact on the US economy and its energy mix has been dramatic. Gas prices in the US dropped from over $13 in 2008 to under $3 in 2016 and the US has moved from a net importer to a net exporter of gas. With cheap gas, both coal and nuclear are less competitive in the US power sector so gas is increasingly displacing the share of coal and nuclear. With less expensive electricity and with gas prices significantly cheaper than in Europe and Japan, energy-intensive manufacturing industry has enjoyed a renaissance. The US shale gas revolution has also had broader international impacts, contributing to the de-linking of gas and oil prices, with LNG imports originally intended for the US being diverted to Asia, and with the glut in US coal supplies, contributing to growing exports and increased coal consumption in Europe, most notably in Germany. Although the US has been at the technological forefront of the 'shale gas revolution', it only possesses the fourth largest reserves of unconventional gas, behind China, Argentina and Algeria. Indeed, the tantalizing promise of unconventional gas is that it might be geographically dispersed in a way similar to coal, and thus conferring on gas the energy security advantages that coal possesses.

There are, though, many political constraints and obstacles to such prospects being realized. In terms of the globalization of gas markets, there is political pressure in the US to preserve its comparative advantage in terms of cheaper energy costs and thus to limit the exports of gas which might potentially damage the US domestic economy. Traditional suppliers, such as Russia, are also likely to resist developments in the structuring of the gas market which are aimed at weakening the bargaining power of the major gas exporters. A global gas price will also not necessarily mean cheap gas and there could be just as much price volatility as with oil. Indeed, an additional potential danger, given the concentration of the key suppliers, is that the development of a global market could result in the formation of a gas cartel which, through restricting supply, would generate greater rents in the industry. The development of the Gas Exporting Countries Forum (GECF) could be the prototype organization for this as it represents some 70 per cent of global natural gas production (Stern 2010). However, there is no sign as yet that such a cartel is emerging.

In relation to the prospect for an expansion of global unconventional gas, Stevens has highlighted the specificities of US social, economic and political conditions which made the 'shale gas revolution' possible (Stevens 2010). It is not clear that such favourable political and economic conditions exist in other parts of the world, which might hope to benefit from unconventional gas. In Europe, a mix of poorer geological conditions, high population densities and stronger environmental pressures have reduced the prospects for exploitation of this resource. In China, water pressures might also limit its ambitions. There is also the danger that over-optimistic assessments of future unconventional gas might deter investment in capital-intensive conventional gas projects which would limit supply in the future. This is particularly the case where such gas is found in politically challenging conditions where a stable investment climate is potentially at risk from resource nationalism and shifts in political governance.

Renewables – a Return to the Past?

Gas might be viewed as an essential 'transition' fuel to a new energy paradigm but it remains a fossil fuel which contributes to greenhouse gas emissions and thus needs eventually to be displaced if climate change is to be averted. Modern renewable energy is increasingly seen as the principal means to ensure an energy future freed both from dependence on fossil fuels and from the perceived dangers of nuclear energy. Renewables are at the core of the vision of a radically reconstituted energy system which uses fuels that are clean, sustainable and yet also support economic development and prosperity. Renewables received their first major impetus in the 1970s with the energy crisis of that period and benefited from the desire to shift away from dependence on oil in power generation. Wind power, for example, first started to become a significant source of energy in the United States during this period (Ball 2012; Shum 2015). The conjunction of high energy prices in the 2000s and the growing concern over climate change has given the modern renewables industry a second major push. In 2015, an estimated 147 GW of renewable power capacity was added, the largest annual increase ever (REN21 2016). Goldman Sachs estimates that the low-carbon economy is now a growing $600bn per annum revenue opportunity with major growth predicted for the period from 2015 to 2025 (Korooshy et al. 2015).

There is something inherently attractive, even romantic, about the promise of modern renewables. There is the visible link to the dominant pre-industrial sources of energy but using the most innovative and modern technologies to enhance their energy efficiency. The modern wind turbine has a clear antecedent with the traditional windmill but also represents a new transformation in a defiantly modernist landscape. This highlights the radical and unprecedented nature of the energy transition that is heralded by the promise of renewables. While previous energy transitions, such as those from traditional organic carriers to coal, or from coal to oil, were transitions from fuels of lower to superior energy densities, the transition to renewables will be in the reverse direction. While currently the fossil fuel-based system is characterized by concentrated energies with high densities, the renewables-based system will have to 'collect fuels of low energy density at low power densities over extensive areas and concentrate them in the increasingly more populous consumption centres' (Smil 2010: 119).

Moving from this vision of the future to the contemporary realities of energy use requires a clearer understanding of how renewables currently fit into the global energy mix. The IEA notes (see figure 6.4) that in 2013 renewables constituted 13.5 per cent of total primary energy supply (TPES), with a 21.6 per cent share of global electricity production (IEA 2015). However, of that 13.5 per cent of energy production, the largest component is the 10.4 per cent share of solid biofuels, of which roughly 8 per cent is traditional biomass used by the world's poorest people to provide basic energy services such as cooking and heating. The remaining 2 per cent of bioenergy includes the more

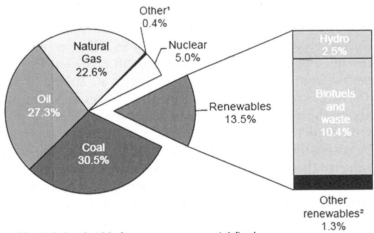

1. Other includes electricity from energy sources not defined
   above such as non-renewable wastes, peat, oil shale and chemical heat.
2. Other renewables includes geothermal, wind, solar, tide.
Note: Totals in graphs might not add up due to rounding.

Figure 6.4   Renewables and Fuel Shares in Total Primary Energy Supply, 2013
Source: © OECD/IEA 2015 Key Renewables Trends (Excerpt from Renewable Information), IEA Publishing. Licence www .iea.org/t&c

modern provision of high-quality energy services – heat, power and transport fuels – that are used primarily in affluent countries (Slade and Bauen 2015). The second largest category of renewables after solid biofuels is that of hydropower, representing 2.5 per cent of world TPES and providing about one fifth of global electricity supplies. The contribution of other modern renewables, including wind, solar, tide and geothermal energy, constitutes 1.3 per cent of TPES. This helps to contextualize the encouraging fast growth in solar photovoltaic (PV) and wind power since 1990, which have grown at an average annual rate of 46.6 per cent and 24.8 per cent respectively. On a global level, production remains relatively small and the overall impact is limited due to the very low starting base.

Closer analysis of this more complex picture of the renewables category also qualifies the image of renewables as inevitably benign. In poorer countries the share of renewables is much greater than in affluent countries with, for example, Africa having a 49.6 per cent share of renewables in its energy mix as against an average of 9 per cent in industrialized countries. This relatively high penetration is, though, an expression of the deep structural inequalities between wealthier societies and their modern energy systems and those poorer parts of the world which suffer energy deprivation due to their reliance on pre-industrial sources of energy. It is estimated that 1.4 billion of the world's poorest lack access to electricity and 2.4 billion rely on traditional woody biomass for cooking (Bhattacharyya 2013: 228). This lack of access to modern energy services increases poverty, with the typical household needing to spend a relatively high cost to purchase these fuels, as well as having to shoulder the associated costs of collecting and using them (Sovacool 2012: 275). Women are particularly vulnerable as they take the largest responsibility for collection of firewood. There are also serious public health consequences, the most significant being due to indoor air pollution with resulting high incidences of child pneumonia, lung cancer and chronic obstructive pulmonary diseases. These health costs are estimated to be responsible for 1.6 million deaths each year (United Nations 2010). Overall, the need to overcome these structural injustices, to ensure that the world's poorest have access to modern energy services, requires a shift from traditional renewables and undoubtedly will include, at least in part, a transition to the energy services provided by fossil fuels.

Just as the progressive image of renewables needs to be qualified, so the environmental benefits are more ambiguous than sometimes assumed. Two examples illustrate this. As already noted, hydropower has a long and distinguished history as a flexible and backup source of electricity that can quickly adapt to changing energy demands. Hydro accounts for one fifth of the world's electricity supply and has helped to shape economic growth in countries like the United States, Canada and Norway (Finlay et al. 2015). The historical path has also been one of increases in the size of dams, starting with Hoover Dam's 1.3 GW power plant built in the US in 1936 to the mammoth 22.5 GW Three Gorges Dam that was opened in China in 2008 (Rai et al. 2014). However, this increase in the size of dams has come with growing criticisms of the environmental and social costs. The Three Gorges Dam displaced an estimated one million people, many of whom received very little in terms of compensation. Large dams pose substantial risks to fish populations, water quality, flow, as well as having potentially negative impacts on the local environment. The power produced by these dams tends to be produced in poor rural areas and is then transported to affluent parts of cities. These social and environmental costs were well-documented in a report by the World Commission on Dams in 2000 (WCD 2000). Warnings have also increased of the negative economic costs of such large dam projects, noting that they typically cost far more than first estimated and can saddle countries with large debts. The overall result of this has been a period of stagnant investment and a critical reassessment of the role of hydropower in development. While hydropower was responsible for 18.1 per cent of world electricity production in 1990, this had reduced to 16.3 per cent by 2013. While developing countries are still investing strongly in hydropower, this is at a significantly lower level than was earlier projected.

A similar trajectory of optimistic projections, followed by awareness of significant social and environmental costs, is also evident in relation to modern biofuels. In the 1990s, bioenergy was regarded as relatively uncontroversial and as a benign alternative to fossil fuels, supporting energy security, mitigation of climate change and agricultural development. At that time, food and energy prices were comparatively low and agricultural land was being taken out of production in Europe and the US so as to avoid food surpluses (Slade and Bauen 2015: 345). Between 2000 and 2010, production quintupled, with biofuels rising from producing 1 per cent to 4 per cent of worldwide transport energy. However, this production of transport fuels from commodity food crops has become increasingly controversial, particularly with the food price spike in 2008. The principal concern was that using food crops in this way increases competition for land, driving up the price of food and leading to a number of other undesirable indirect effects, including potentially increasing greenhouse gas emissions through the conversion of pasture and forested land to arable production. There was also evidence that agricultural lobbies in the US and EU were engaged in capturing rent against the interests of the consumers who consequently suffer from increased food prices and food price volatility (Eide 2008; Bailey 2013). Although investment in bioenergy is projected to increase in the future, with the IEA predicting an increase from the current 2 per cent to 8 per cent of world road-transport fuel demand being met by biofuels by 2035, there is much greater consciousness of the social and environmental complexities of sourcing large amounts of biomass for energy production.

The cases of large-scale hydropower and biofuels show that it is not just nuclear energy which can suffer from unexpected social, political and environmental shifts in mood that substantially change perceptions and undermine earlier optimistic forecasts. Such complexity and volatility needs to be taken into consideration when considering the prospective fortunes of wind and solar power, which are generally viewed as currently holding great promise and are receiving the most investor interest. Wind and solar energy offer clear advantages over fossil fuels in that they are clean sources of energy that do not emit the carbon dioxide that contributes to climate change nor the pollutants that cause smog. There has been particularly fast growth in wind power which developed rapidly in the EU during the 2000s; other countries, such as the US, China and India, are now catching up. Wind power currently generates 1.7 per cent of global electricity generation but, with its 25 per cent annual growth rate, has considerable potential for the future. Solar energy starts with a significantly lower base of only generating 0.1 per cent of the world's electricity but its potential is theoretically even greater than that of wind. The sun produces an almost limitless supply of energy and is also easily distributed, with PV panels being able to be placed almost anywhere rather than the stationary concentrations of wind turbines required for generating sizeable amounts of wind power.

Estimates for the future economic potential for wind and solar power vary substantially depending on different expectations of technology costs, levels of subsidies and degree of public acceptability. Within the various IEA scenarios, for example, the contribution of wind to global electricity production varies between 5 and 18 per cent by 2050 (Ball 2012). There have undoubtedly been major advances in reduction in production costs and introduction of new efficient technologies for both wind and solar energy. There is, thus, much cause for expectation of continued fast growth and penetration.

However, there remain significant obstacles and constraints that need to be overcome if wind and solar are fully to realize their potential. There is, first, the fact that both the sun and wind are intermittent sources of energy and are unevenly distributed. Critically, they lack the entrenched infrastructures that exist for electricity production using fossil fuels. There are, as a consequence, very large costs to integrate wind and solar into the electricity grid with the need in most countries for substantial new transmission lines to be built from the generally under-populated areas where these energy sources are concentrated to the main centres of population. For example, it is estimated that Germany will need to build 3,800 km of new power lines, incurring a cost of €10–27bn by 2020, to support its ambitions for the transformation of its electricity system through integration of renewables (Dodds and Fais 2015: 438–9). All of this has a significant impact on power markets with many utilities, such as in Europe, having a crisis of profitability. There is also the challenge to develop energy storage capacity for low-carbon systems, which rely on the high penetration of intermittent renewables. Super-grids, such as those proposed for Europe, which could connect with North Africa and its potential for solar energy, represent major challenges, not least in relation to energy security concerns. There is also a fundamental question of cost and the reality that, like nuclear, there are substantial front-end capital costs for low-carbon systems, such as wind and solar energy. The social and political acceptability for this is not a foregone conclusion. It is notable that the EU's ambitious lead in developing renewables was severely challenged by the 2008 economic crisis, with concerns for economic competitiveness leading to the reduction or withdrawal of a number of subsidies for the renewables industry (Bressand 2012: 50).

Overall, what can be drawn from this general analysis is that significant advances have been made in promoting modern renewables, with wind turbines, solar panels and biofuels being much cheaper and more competitive than before. However, the overall movement remains incremental rather than revolutionary. The renewables energy revolution might take place in the future but that course is not yet set. Rather, the current dynamic, at the global and regional level, is more modest and it is primarily driven by the need to accommodate new demand in both the developed and developing world rather than to phase out fossil fuel use. Renewables are certainly a growing piece of the energy pie, but their role at the present time is to supplement rather than replace the current energy mix.

Conclusion

This chapter has examined the differing markets and political economies of the major energy fuels and flows – coal, oil, nuclear, gas and renewables. The main focus has been on the interlinkage between energy and economic security, examining each of these fuels in turn. The overarching picture is of states, driven by concerns about both energy security and economic competitiveness, seeking to preserve and expand their portfolio of energy sources to meet expectant future demand. There is limited evidence as yet of states seeking radically to displace fossil fuels on environmental grounds if this incurs very significant economic or security costs. There are certainly individual cases, such as the UK's decision to phase out coal power generation, that do indicate a commitment in this direction. But, in the US, the closure of coal power stations is driven as much by the relative cost competitiveness of gas as by strictly environmental activism.

A prime example of this hold of fossil fuels is coal's survival as a major global fuel. The global growth in demand over the past two decades reflects its clear advantages in terms of both energy and economic security. It is both widely distributed geographically and is relatively cheap. This has preserved its use in power generation in particular. Future growth is projected to come from the developing world with a contrasting decline in developed countries. The continuing attraction of coal for industrialization in the developing world also highlights the importance of justice considerations in the energy choices that states make. For China and India, as well as other fast developing countries, coal continues to be perceived as essential for the transition to modernity and to ensure access to the energy services that affluent countries currently enjoy. To deny this on environmental grounds is perceived as an expression of historical injustice.

Oil presents a different case. It differs from coal in that it raises both serious energy security anxieties, as addressed in other parts of this book, as well as economic security concerns with volatile and, at times, very high prices. Oil has, as a consequence, been substituted by other fuels in a number of sectors, most notably in the power industry. However, oil's practical advantages in terms of fuelling global transportation remain overwhelming, with its retention of a 95 per cent market share of the transportation sector. Progress in terms of substitution has thus been limited to date, preserving oil's share of the global energy mix. Given the large economic infrastructures, and the social and political embeddedness of the global oil-fuelled contemporary civilization, ensuring the secure supply of oil remains a priority for states in terms of economic security. Citizens in all states value the personal freedom conferred by modern transport and governments are judged by their success in ensuring this.

Nuclear, natural gas and renewables have all been developed so as potentially to break or weaken the dependence on coal and oil and their associated energy security and environmental costs. While each has gained a significant share in the total primary energy supply, none has yet realized their original expected potential. Nuclear's early promise was never realized as energy security anxieties grew over the safety of nuclear power and its linkages to weapons production. Its economic competitiveness also declined over time. While nuclear's fortunes declined, natural gas has experienced a certain renaissance, particularly through the expansion of the international LNG trade and the exploitation of unconventional gas. However, there remain multiple political, social and economic constraints which need to be overcome, particularly because, like oil, gas raises significant energy security anxieties as well as being a fossil fuel and thus responsible for greenhouse gas emissions. Renewables represent the most recent promise of an energy future that is freed from the pollution generated by fossil fuels and the perceived dangers of nuclear power. But there remain many complex economic and technological challenges to convert what are inherently lower energy and power densities of renewables flows into fuels or electricity.

The end result is that states, confronted by increased complexity and diversity in energy systems and facing conflicting and often irreconcilable societal interests, have opted to keep their options open, not least as a means of ensuring both energy security and international competitiveness. Whether this approach is adequate to meet the environmental challenges of the future, most notably in relation to climate change, is the subject of the next chapter.

– 7 –
Energy Security and Sustainability

This chapter assesses the risks and threats that the contemporary global energy system poses for the sustainability of our environment. The key issue that the chapter addresses is whether the historical drive for ensuring energy security, based as it has primarily been on gaining access to non-renewable fossil fuels, is a sustainable process and whether it might be gradually 'sowing the seeds of its own destruction', leading to some serious and even catastrophic end.

Two specific threats or future-oriented scenarios will be assessed. The first is the claim that there are physical limits to the extent to which fossil fuels can be extracted since they are depletable and non-renewable resources. The most prominent argument for this is the heavily contested claim that we are reaching, or have already reached, a peak of production for conventional oil and that the future will involve a decline in its supply. Although the 'peak oil' debate has been the most vigorous, similar projections have been made for other fuels, such as gas and coal, as well as other minerals. The second threat is the claim, for which there is much greater scientific consensus, that the cumulative and growing emissions of carbon dioxide and other greenhouse gases, for which the burning of fossil fuels is the most significant contributor, is leading to a global warming of the planet which will have serious and unpredictable negative consequences for future human well-being and for the global ecosystems that underpin our contemporary civilization.

The articulation of these potentially highly damaging threats presents a serious challenge to what has been called earlier the 'modernizing narrative' of our fossil-fuelled industrial civilization. This narrative highlights how human life has been transformed, making it more prosperous, more expansive, freer and more secure. As noted in the previous chapter, most developing countries seeking to bring their populations out of poverty still view their route to prosperity as relying upon the use of fossil fuels, including the most pollutant, coal. This modernizing narrative also emphasizes the innate human capacities for ingenuity, innovation and cooperation to find solutions to problems which might appear to be otherwise intractable.

The alternative more critical narrative, reflected in the projections for peak oil and climate change, challenges this optimism and argues that there are limits and constraints to such exponential growth and that a radical re-thinking of the fundamental underpinning of our fossil fuel-based civilization needs to be undertaken.

It is not surprising that, with such radically differing narratives, simple and mutually agreed solutions to avert these potential future threats have not been easy to reach. Although this chapter argues that the claim that we are running out of fossil fuels is misconceived, this does not mean that a 'peak oil' or 'peak coal' will not eventually be reached. However, this is likely to be driven more by demand than supply factors, linked to the need to reduce the emissions that cause global warming. However, this drive to reduce emissions has, so far, had limited success due to the failure to reach a full agreement on an effective and comprehensive plan of action to avert climate change. The record of over two decades of negotiations over climate change, initiated by the UN Framework

Convention on Climate Change signed in 1992 at the Rio Earth summit, has notably failed to reduce the emissions of greenhouse gases into the atmosphere, making it increasingly more difficult to limit the increase in the global temperature.

Why this is the case provides us with critical insights into the complex and conflictual relationship between energy security and sustainability. It offers an underlying context for understanding why it has been difficult to get states to agree upon a comprehensive, legally enforceable agreement when there are so many differing interests, values and perspectives to be reconciled. It is not just a question of conflicting narratives but also, as the key theme of this book argues, about differing and competing values of what constitutes a just and sustainable agreement, particularly in relation to such a complex phenomenon as climate change. Energy security and environmental sustainability are two key contested values but these are not the only ones; there are also the competing values of economic efficiency and prosperity and the deeply historically engrained legacies of unequal power relations and competing claims for justice. The chapter will conclude by highlighting that, though there are grounds for pessimism for the future, there are also reasons for some optimism, though these are more evident in incremental and discontinuous steps and rely upon a continuing hope and expectation of the powers of human ingenuity, innovation and cooperation. Whether these will be sufficient to avert the threats posed by climate change is something only the future can tell us.

Neo-Malthusianism and Peak Oil

Behind the peak oil debate, there lies a longer historical tradition that sees unrestrained human activities as inexorably leading to a severe deterioration in the environment with potentially disastrous implications for human welfare. This tradition has sometimes been defined as neo-Malthusian in deference to Thomas Malthus, the economist and demographer of the late eighteenth century, who was one of the first to highlight the dangers of population growth outstripping food production. His basic argument was that human misery and hardship were inevitable because the human population was growing exponentially while food production was only growing linearly (Malthus 2003 [1820]). This notion of exponential growth was popularized for the modern era in the Club of Rome's classic *Limits to Growth* (Meadows et al. 1972). The report argued that in five key areas – population, food production, industrialization, pollution and consumption of non-renewable resources – there was clear evidence of unsustainable exponential growth from one year to the next, which could be understood metaphorically as a process of 'doubling time'. In an associated body of research, linked in particular to the work of Thomas Homer-Dixon, the resulting cumulative environmental constraints have, it is argued, led to a 'tipping point' or an environmental 'threshold' which is feeding into increased violence and conflict over access to diminishing resources (Homer-Dixon and Blitt 1998; Homer-Dixon 2001).

It is important to note that non-renewable resources, including fossil fuels, are only one dimension of this more comprehensive and interconnected resource scarcity nexus. However, anxieties over our dependence on fossil fuels have been a major catalyst for these broader concerns. It was the energy crisis of the 1970s, and the economic recession that this caused, which provided the background to the work of the Club of Rome and gave a general boost to the emergent environmental movement. There is also a tradition, which can be traced back to the revulsion against the soot and grime caused by the use of coal in seventeenth-century London, that presents our use of fossil fuels as dehumanizing and destructive. On a more political level, the belief that national power is dependent on what are ultimately finite resources has been a recurrent source of anxiety. In the nineteenth century, the leading British economist Stanley Jevons worried about the prospect of an imminent scarcity of coal supplies and feared that, without quickly finding substitutes, 'Britain might contract to its former littleness' (Jevons 2008 [1865]: 236).

Jevons's 'peak coal' prefigures the more recent 'peak oil' thesis. The main advocates for this thesis, represented by the Association for the Study of Peak Oil (ASPO), put forward three main claims: the extraction rate for conventional oil supplies is nearing its global maximum; this imminent peak will result in a permanent shortage relative to demand; and this will lead to a powerful oil shock and the permanent 'end of cheap oil' (Campbell and Laherrere 1998). The intellectual roots for this thesis are found in the statistically-based model of oil depletion developed by the geologist Marion King Hubbert in the 1950s in relation to US production (Deffeyes 2001). His model indicates that unrestrained oil production peaks when roughly half the reserves in a region have been extracted. The plausibility for this was strengthened by the accuracy of his prediction for US conventional oil production. Extrapolating this model globally, peak oil advocates argue that, taking the most reliable figures for oil extraction globally over the last 150 years along with the best assessments of remaining reserves, the maximum rate of extraction, the point at which there is an 'oil peak', will occur sometime between 2010 and 2025. Empirically, supporting evidence for this is found in how few large oil fields are being discovered, the declines in production of existing large fields, and the fact that many oil regions, such as the North Sea, have demonstrated similar 'peaks' as occurred in the United States (Bridge 2010; Criqui 2013).

The 'peak oil' thesis has been taken to corroborate the predictions of increasing geopolitical and military confrontation over energy resources from leading scholars on both the left and right (Klare 2001; Harvey 2003; Mitchell 2011). It has also been a key argument for the urgent call to wean ourselves off fossil fuels and move to renewables

(Hopkins 2014; Schneider-Mayerson 2015). However, there are also influential critics of the thesis, mainly social scientists rather than geologists, who argue that the peak oil advocates focus at the 'below-ground' physical and geological at the expense of 'above-ground' social, economic and political factors. For these critics, it is these 'above-ground' factors that are ultimately more critical in determining the degree of access and the extent of extraction of valuable resources like oil. It is, in particular, the vital roles that markets, ingenuity, technological innovation and the capacity for substitution that must, on this analysis, be factored in to provide a more realistic and holistic approach (Lynch 2003; Adelman 2004; Odell 2010).

This more socio-economic and political approach qualifies a number of the assumptions of the 'peak oil' thesis. The first is that we can have such a clear quantifiable knowledge of the total resource base when recoverable oil reserves are not a static or independently known quantity but rather a function of various complex factors, including technological knowledge, governmental policies and, most importantly, the price of oil (Lynch 1996). This is evident in the ways that oil price rises over the last three decades, which have frequently been interpreted as confirming the peak oil thesis, have subsequently been shown to be primarily due to the temporary lack of investment for economic or political reasons rather than as a result of reaching a geological limit. Thus, the oil price rises in the 1970s led to international oil companies energetically investing in the discovery and bringing into production of oil fields in the non-OPEC world, most notably in the North Sea and Gulf of Mexico. Similarly, the oil price rises in the 2000s led to a geographical expansion of new oil fields in different parts of the world, such as in Brazil, Canada, Alaska, the Black Sea and different parts of Africa. Even more significantly, substantial non-conventional oil and gas reserves have been developed, most notably in the United States, through the unexpected convergence of three distinctive technological innovations: fracking; horizontal drilling techniques; and seismic information technologies (Helm 2012: 140–5).

The failure to give sufficient weight to the importance of the role of technological innovation is a second significant weakness in the peak oil thesis. This affects, for example, the whole issue of recovery rates for existing oil fields. It is commonly considered that the average recovery rate is currently around 35 per cent. Even a small increase in the recovery rate adds considerably to accounted reserves even without discoveries. Some consider that the recovery rate could be as high as 60 per cent 50 years from now, which transforms estimates for recoverable reserves (Criqui 2013: 195). The third factor qualifying the peak oil thesis is the failure to incorporate the potential for substitution. Even if a peak in conventional oil supplies occurs, the potential for non-conventional sources to compensate for this needs to be included. Also, it is not oil *per se* which is required for the energy services that it supports, such as road transportation, but rather the 'liquid energy' that it provides. Both gas and coal, for which there are very large reserves, can be converted to the liquid fuel required. In addition, substitution can take the form of cars being powered by electricity which again would reduce the demand for oil. When all of this is accounted for, the ultimate reserves for 'liquid fuels' are more than sufficient for a long time ahead, as figure 7.1 demonstrates.

As against the thrust of the 'peak oil' thesis, the reality is that there is more than enough fossil fuel for a considerable period ahead and that we are unlikely to run out at any point soon. But this does not mean that talking of peaks is irrelevant. It is already possible to see that in the OECD countries a 'peak demand' has occurred in relation to oil. The peak was reached in 2004–5 and the demand for oil has been in decline since, reflecting the general reductions in demand for energy among post-industrial states. In addition, if there is going to be any even partial success in averting the dangers of climate change, there has

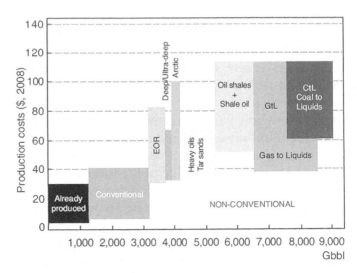

Figure 7.1 Conventional and Non-Conventional Liquid Hydrocarbons
Source: IFP Energies nouvelles (2012) 'Non-conventional hydrocarbons: evolution or revolution', *Panorama 2012*, available at: http://www.ifpenergiesnouvelles.fr/Actualites/Evenements/ Nous-organisons/Panorama-2012/(language)/fre-FR

to be a 'peak demand' for at least the most pollutant fossil fuels, such as oil and coal. Modelling of a 'global regime', where there is full global compliance with limiting climate change, projected oil consumption is set to decline from about 95 million barrels per day in 2020 to 61 million barrels per day in 2050 (Criqui 2013: 202). The implications of this have led to a growing recognition that many resource-rich countries with substantial oil, gas and coal supplies might end up being 'stranded assets' that these countries will have to leave in the ground and will not be able to exploit (McGlade and Ekins 2015). The former Saudi oil minister, Shaykh Yamani, captured this rather different way of conceiving of peaks by noting that 'the stone age did not end when people ran out of stones' and that the same will be the case with the 'oil age'. The recent aggressive Saudi strategy to maintain market share by not reducing, as it has done in the past, its production when oil demand and prices dropped rapidly in 2014, indicates that this longer-term strategic concern is incorporated in its current strategic calculation.

A final reflection on peaks is that it is not just fossil fuels that might reach their 'peak' but that it is important also to consider the prospect of a 'renewables peak'. The fact that the sun, wind and water are ever-present and indefinitely renewable does not mean that their ubiquity can be translated into limitless energy supplies despite claims to the contrary (for an optimistic assessment, see Jacobson and Delucchi 2011; for a more sceptical position, see Trainer 2007). There are, in practice, multiple constraints against such expansion, particularly if the ambition is to move rapidly beyond the current marginal role of renewables in global energy supply. These constraints include geographical limits, including large tracts of the world not suitable for solar and wind energy as well as public opposition to such developments; the technical constraints that make it expensive to produce the energy or where the energy return on the amount invested (EROI) is not sufficient to be viable; the energy security concerns that would come from the internationalization of renewable energy, such as transmitting solar-generated electricity from North Africa to Europe, crossing borders in the ways that oil and gas currently do; and the constraints on ensuring that renewable energy production does not negatively affect other vital ecosystems, such as water supply or agricultural land, a problem that was discussed in the previous chapter in relation to hydropower and biofuels (Moriarty and Honnery 2016). There are also the problems with the intermittency of much renewable sources, such as wind and solar, and the additional costs that this creates in terms of the expansion of the grid, building over-capacity and in developing additional storage capacities. Overall, this means that the notion of a 'peak' to renewables production is not to be discounted simply because these sources are 'renewable' (Anderson 2015).

Energy Security and Climate Change

While the peak oil thesis has at times captured the public imagination, this is nothing compared to climate change, which has undoubtedly become the most critical environmental issue affecting international relations and contemporary global energy policies. However, it is important to stress that the issue of climate change, and the associated need to transform our energy systems, is only one dimension of a complex multi-faceted set of environmental challenges. As well as climate change, there are other important interconnected environmental challenges, such as the problems of water scarcity affecting many parts of the world; the widescale deforestation that is critically contributing to the loss of biodiversity; the problem of food shortages and hunger and poverty; and the continuing challenge of population growth, as the world's population is still on a fast growth pattern with an expected population of over nine billion in 2050 as against the roughly seven billion in 2016 (Andrews-Speed et al. 2012; Dannreuther 2013: 140).

Despite the seriousness of these various environmental and socio-economic challenges, climate change has gained a pre-eminence, at least symbolically and rhetorically, as the key environmental issue of our age. Part of the reason for this is a question of timing, as the initial period of heightened climate change concerns coincided with the ending of the Cold War in the late 1980s. With the loss of the existential threat of a nuclear conflagration, climate change, and its associated severe environmental and human consequences, offered an alternative existential threat for the future. This also fed into the arguments of that time of the need to shift security away from its focus on war and violence to that of the environment and other non-traditional threats (Mathews 1989; Prins 1990; Myers 1993). At the same time, there emerged a strong network of scientists and environmental policy experts who converged on a scientific consensus that climate change was definitely happening, that it was primarily due to human activities, and that action needed to be taken to avert the potential disastrous consequences for human well-being (Haas 1990; Miller and Edwards 2001).

The sense that climate change was a clearly defined global problem that needed a global solution was also one that fitted into the dominant post-Cold War paradigm of globalization and the need for enhanced international cooperation. At the same time, there was a recent precedent for what such an environmental agreement should look like: the Montreal Protocol on Substances that Deplete the Ozone Layer that was signed in 1987. This Protocol is generally regarded as one of the most successful international environmental agreements ever. It has resulted in worldwide consumption of ozone-depleting substances falling by over 90 per cent between 1986 and 2004; the depletion of stratospheric ozone over Antarctica stabilizing and being reversed; and projections of a recovery back to 1980 levels to be achieved by 2050 (Benedick 1998; Velders et al. 2007).

With the optimism generated by the success of the Montreal Protocol, it is perhaps not surprising that a similar approach was adopted to seek to deal with the need to radically reduce greenhouse gas emissions so as to limit global warming (Hulme 2009: 291–3). Theoretically, the international climate change framework conforms to a 'regime theory' model with functionalist and liberal institutionalist understandings of international cooperation (Keohane and Nye 1977; Krasner 1983). The key underlying assumption is that divergent national interests can be reconciled into an international agreement through an iterative process of negotiation so long as there is a commitment to an overarching set of norms and principles, the assurance of information transparency, the establishment of effective monitoring and review processes, and the establishment of enforcement mechanisms to deal with non-compliance. A key area of difference with realist and more sceptical approaches to international cooperation is that regime theory assumes that states are willing to forego relative gains, such as their relative position in the international system, in exchange for the absolute gains that all states will benefit from the agreement (Grieco 1988). Most of the literature on the climate change regime has tended to follow this more optimistic view on the conditions for international cooperation (Young 2010; Vogler 2016: 6).

The global climate change regime that subsequently emerged from this process incorporates a complex and sophisticated set of institutions. The regime is founded on two legally binding treaties – the 1992 United Nations Framework Convention on Climate Change (UNFCCC) and its 1997 Kyoto Protocol – and a host of other decisions, guidelines and procedures adopted by parties to these treaties (Depledge 2015). The Conference of the Parties (COP) is the main political decision-making body of the regime and the regime is driven by continuous intergovernmental negotiations, held at least twice a year. The Kyoto Protocol was the key international agreement within the climate change regime that committed its parties to internationally binding emission reduction targets. The key ambition and purpose of the regime is to 'stabilize atmospheric concentrations of greenhouse gases at a level that would avoid dangerous anthropogenic interference with the climate system' (Article 2).

There are three notable features in the evolution of the global climate change regime. The first is that an agreement on clear measures to quantify the overarching ambition was slow to emerge. It was only in 2009, over ten years after Kyoto, that an agreement was finally reached to hold the increase in global average temperature to below 2°C above pre-industrial levels. Current scientific estimates of how to achieve this requires overall concentrations of CO_2 emissions to be limited to 450 ppm; to achieve greater likelihood of success, the levels would have to be even less, possibly as low as 400 ppm. Although there has been a general convergence on this 2°C target, some particularly vulnerable states, such as the Association of Small Island States (AOSIS), have argued that a 1.5°C target is required to avert extremely damaging environmental consequences. This ambition was included in the final agreements of the 2015 Paris COP. The scale of this ambition is seen in the fact that current concentrations of CO_2 emissions are currently estimated already to have breached 400 ppm and, even with no increases in rates of emissions, will reach 550 ppm by 2050.

The second feature is that the commitments reached for emissions reductions through the Kyoto Protocol have generally been relatively modest. One factor behind this was the decision made in the early 1990s to divide the regime's parties between the developed and the developing world. It was only the developed countries, those designated as such in the Protocol's Annex I, who made quantified commitments, originally agreeing to a collective 5 per cent cut from 1990 levels by 2012. The non-Annex I parties, which included large emerging countries like China with its rapidly rising emissions, refused until recently to even consider making any such quantifiable commitments. The regime's credibility also suffered a major defeat in 2001 when the United States rejected the Kyoto Protocol, citing in particular the lack of commitment of the large existing non-Annex I emitters such as China.

The third feature of the Kyoto Protocol is how it has promoted and supported instruments for emissions trading as well as the general development of national and regional carbon markets. Within the regime, this includes such mechanisms as joint implementation where Annex I countries are permitted to have low-carbon projects in one developed country generate emissions credits in another country; and the Clean Development Mechanism (CDM) which does the same between Annex I and non-Annex I countries. The CDM has been the principal way through which developing countries have been involved in the regime, with Annex I parties funding emission-curbing projects in these countries. The Kyoto Protocol regime has also managed carbon trading markets between its parties, the most significant of which has been the European Trading System that developed among the EU member states (Antes et al. 2011; Newell et al. 2013). The ambition of these carbon trading systems is to assign property rights for greenhouse gas emissions and establish a market for the trading in these rights, which would provide clearly defined market incentives to put right what the Stern Review called the 'greatest market failure that the world has ever seen' (Stern 2006).

Despite all this energetic diplomacy and innovative policy, the actual outcomes and results have so far been distinctly disappointing. The reality is that, during the period of the regime, greenhouse gas emissions increased rather than decreased and the rate of annual increase has actually been significantly higher for the period 2000–10, with a 2.2 per cent average annual growth, than for the preceding three decades, when there was an average annual 1.3 per cent growth in emissions (see figure 7.2). More optimistically, there is now an expectation that a peak in emissions might have been reached in 2015 when, for the first time, there was an actual fall in global emissions, mainly due to the decline of coal consumption in China (Jackson et al. 2016). However, this reduction might also be only temporary, particularly if coal consumption increases in other fast industrializing countries in Asia, such as India.

In any case, even if a turning point has been reached, we are very far from limiting climate warming to the 2°C target. To achieve this, there is a need for a 50 per cent reduction of global emissions from their current levels by 2050. Emissions from industrialized countries would need to be reduced by 80 per cent. Overall, the 2°C target is ambitious and there are real questions whether there is the underlying political will to achieve these commitments. As Patt notes, the challenge of the target is that it makes clear

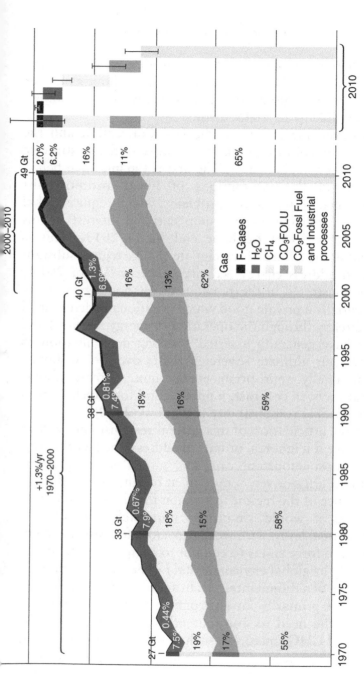

Figure 7.2 Total Annual Anthropogenic GHG Emission by Gases, 1970–2010
Source: IPCC (2014) *Climate Change 2014: Mitigation of Climate Change*. Contribution of Working Group III to the Fifth Assessment. Report of the Intergovernmental Panel on Climate Change [Edenhofer, O., R. Pichs-Madruga, Y. Sokona, E. Farahani, S. Kadner, K. Seyboth, A. Adler, I. Baum, S. Brunner, P. Eickemeier, B. Kriemann, J. Savolainen, S. Schlömer, C. von Stechow, T. Zwickel and J. C. Minx (eds.)]. Cambridge and New York: Cambridge University Press

that 'there is no room for delay' and that we must 'eliminate all net GHG emissions, everywhere, about as fast as
anyone believes politically, economically and technologi-
cally feasible' (Patt 2015: 296).

However, the failure of the UN Convention and the
Kyoto Protocol to make a major impact on this strategic
goal has two main causes. The first is the mistaken belief,
inherent in the assumptions of liberal-institutionalist
regime theory, that global problems, which require global
solutions, will inevitably trump national interests (Prins
and Rayner 2007; Keohane and Victor 2013). This is
evident in the failure of the climate change regime substantially to address energy security concerns (Victor 2011).
As demonstrated in the previous chapter, energy security
is essentially a private good which is nationally determined
(if indirectly through the operation of energy markets) and
states have generally asserted a strong determination to
ensure their ultimate sovereign rights over, for example,
the nationally appropriate energy mix. Climate change
mitigation is, in contrast, a public good for which there is
general global responsibility (Luft et al. 2010).

But the articulation of this general responsibility will be
ineffective if it ignores, or fails to address, the fact that one
of the most important causes of global warming is the
energy security-driven commitment to burning fossil fuels.
The silence of the regime in relation to this is not unintentional as it would simply be impossible for such an
international body, with weak capacities for ensuring compliance, to force states to commit to energy policies driven
primarily by global environmental rather than the complex
balancing of national interests. In addition, defining climate
change as primarily an environmental problem has also
avoided the need to confront other root causes for the
growth of GHG emissions, such as population growth and
the commitment to global economic growth, which similarly encroach upon jealously guarded state prerogatives
(Helm 2012; Vogler 2016). But the consequence is a global
regime to mitigate climate change which is constrained

from directly addressing the core underlying roots of the problem.

The second problem with the regime is the failure to recognize the difficulty of requiring states to make substantial costly commitments for benefits that are not equally distributed or always clearly identifiable. For some states, like the oil-producing states of OPEC or Russia, the costs of a decarbonized world appear much more as an economic cost rather than a prospective gain. In contrast, for the small low-lying island states, the threat of climate change is truly life-threatening. It makes sense for these countries that immediate dramatic action is taken to ensure their future survival. However, such a strong commitment to incur current costs for the sake of future benefits, which potentially privileges future generations against the current one, is not evident among many states, including some of the most significant emitters. For emerging countries like China and India, climate change is essentially viewed as a development problem which will be resolved once they have made the transition to becoming developed countries and, in supporting this transition, they reserve the right to use those resources, such as coal and other fossil fuels, that drive their industrialization and that earlier drove the industrialization processes in the already developed world.

If this development argument is accepted, this leaves the responsibility to the developed countries, who are also the 'historic' emitters, to make the cuts required to mitigate the effects of climate change. This was, in practice, institutionalized at Kyoto through the distinction between Annex I and non-Annex I countries and with the recognition of their differential responsibilities. But this had the knock-on effect of a number of developed countries, most notably the United States, arguing that the regime permitted 'free-riding' from countries who were significantly contributing to the growth in GHG emissions, such as China. Other OECD countries also effectively withdrew from the regime once it became clear that their own emissions were not falling as fast as they had originally committed. Even among the most faithful supporters of the regime, such as the EU states, it is notable that enthusiasm declined as Europe's economic competitiveness became threatened after the 2008 financial crash (Bressand 2013). The reality of the commitments made were also not as demanding as they might seem. For a deindustrializing Europe, it was relatively easy to meet the targets as they were defined in terms of the reduction of territorially-based carbon production from industries and factories that had become redundant, rather than in terms of European carbon consumption, such as embodied in imported manufactured goods from countries such as China, which actually has increased overall.

But even the Kyoto process and the relatively unambitious attempt at obtaining an international, comprehensive and legally binding agreement proved ultimately too much in a world of sovereign states. At the 2015 Paris COP, it was agreed that a comprehensive agreement could only be based on a principle of sovereign voluntariness where the assurance of commitments would at most be through external monitoring and peer pressure rather than through any formal legal compliance mechanisms. The victory of this looser and more devolved approach, where each state makes its own commitments to the global regime through nationally appropriate mitigation actions (NAMAs), has the advantage of including parties who had withdrawn from or been passive in the regime, most notably the United States and China. It has also meant that many developing country emitters have pledged concrete emissions reductions for the first time. However, extending a permissive voluntary model excludes the potential for sanctions or other means of enforcement for states that fail to meet their commitments. The prospects of the regime depend a lot on the expectation that peer review and mutual 'shaming', based on clearly defined metrics and effective monitoring and verification procedures, will keep states to their commitments. An even more challenging condition is that the sum total of these commitments will be sufficient to meet the 2°C target for limiting the increase in the world's temperature.

All of this highlights the reality that the issue of managing climate change mitigation and adaptation raises very significant conflicts over core values. The value of environmental sustainability is a value that all states can in principle agree to as well as, in general, recognizing the seriousness of the threat posed by climate change. But this value competes with the value accorded to security, particularly in relation to energy security, as well as the values of prosperity and economic efficiency. There are also very divergent perspectives linked to legacies of unequal power relations, equity and historical justice. A key aspect of this is the lack of a consensus about who exactly is responsible for global warming. Is it the responsibility of the historical emitters, the industrialized world, who have contributed most to cumulative concentrations of GHG emissions and whose per capita emissions are still very high? Or is it the responsibility of those countries who are currently the largest emitters and thus currently most responsible for the rise in emissions? The United States and a number of other industrialized countries have refused to acknowledge historical responsibilities without taking into account current realities, arguing for the need for a 'level playing field'. Emerging economies, like China and India, have been adamant in highlighting the need to incorporate principles of equity and historical justice (Shue 1995, 1999; Elliot 2006).

Similarly, there is the fundamental and unresolved question of whether it is the primary responsibility of the current generation to resolve the problem of climate change or whether it is reasonable to leave that responsibility to succeeding and, given projected economic growth, richer generations. The Stern Review argued that we should generally treat those future generations essentially equally to the current generation. This was a key element supporting the argument to take swift and decisive action to mitigate climate change, as it would also be cheaper to deal with the problem now rather than leave it for later. But other economists, such as William Nordhaus, argued against Stern on the basis that we generally do not act on behalf of future generations at the expense of the current generation (Hulme 2009; Nordhaus and Shellenberger 2010). The controversial Danish economist, Bjorn Lomborg, argued on similar grounds that, given the large costs to deal with climate change which would primarily benefit future generations, it was preferable to spend these sums on resolving some of the immediate social and economic problems, such as poverty and disease in regions like Sub-Saharan Africa (Lomborg 2004: 236–304).

Grounds for Pessimism or Optimism?

It is not difficult to conclude from the limited effectiveness of the international efforts towards developing an effective climate change regime that a degree of pessimism is justified towards any expectation of averting the substantial dangers of global warming. There is little evidence, for example, that at a fundamental societal and individual level there is a sufficient recognition that substantial energy reductions are required, particularly among citizens in the rich developed world who continue to enjoy extremely high, if not excessive, levels of per capita energy use (Smil 2010: 105). In these rich countries, significant progress has been made in enhancing energy efficiency but this is often cancelled out by the lack of a commensurate decrease in energy use. Indeed, these energy efficiency improvements often have the opposite effect. For example, in the United Kingdom the temperature in the average house has increased from 13°C to 18°C from the 1970s to the present day (Helm 2012: 103). Similarly, the fast growth in personal electronic gadgets has also greatly increased energy use. Overall, this illustrates a core underlying problem that promotion of economic growth is almost universally taken as an overriding objective, even among the most developed countries, and such growth frequently leads to increased, rather than reduced, energy consumption.

When this drive for economic growth is translated into the ambition for poorer developing countries to be wealthy and prosperous, then the pressures on ensuring an effective climate change regime become even greater. As was noted in the previous chapter, the emerging economies are determined to make their citizens more prosperous, to have more energy-demanding 'Western' lifestyles, and will strongly resist any external pressure to deny them the right of access to fossil fuels. In reality, the most important cause of the significant increase in emissions from 2000 to 2010 was China's economic boom, which was driven by its extensive use of fossil fuels, most notably its domestic coal supplies as well as large-scale imports of oil, coal and gas. If India or other large developing countries were to follow the resource-intensive path of China, even to a limited degree, the impact on global emissions would only intensify. In general, the pent-up demand for energy services among developing countries, particularly if the overriding objective is economic growth, can only currently be conceivable with a large expansion in the use of fossil fuels, with the concomitant impacts on climate change.

Another factor which also fosters a degree of pessimism is the embedded reality of the current $20 trillion fossil fuel energy complex. There is an extensive literature which highlights the ways in which technological lock-in occurs, favouring existing systems even if they are less efficient or effective than alternative systems (David 1985; Arthur 1994; LaBelle and Horwitch 2013). Such path dependencies are further strengthened by institutional lock-in, where governments and other actors, including consumer groups, resist and discourage the adoption of new innovations, and old inefficient technologies remain in place (Unruh 2000; Andrews-Speed 2016). However, as noted in the previous chapter, the existing fossil fuel energy systems are generally quite efficient, in strictly economic terms, compared to the currently available renewable alternatives.

The infrastructure of the fossil fuel systems is one of generally highly centralized extraction, with fuels incorporating high energy and power densities, and which support well the increasingly high density urbanization processes; the modern renewables systems are, in contrast, generally more decentralized, with lower energy and power densities, and work less efficiently in large cities. Making the transition away from fossil fuel systems thus requires a much more difficult transition than previous energy transitions, such as from coal to oil-based systems, since it is driven by environmental rather than economic factors.

The prospect of public opposition to such a transition should also not be underestimated. It is salutary to note how optimistic projections for carbon-free or low-carbon energy sources have disappointed in the past. This includes the public disillusionment in relation to nuclear energy and to hydropower, which resulted in significantly lower expectations for future growth in these low-carbon technologies. Similar opposition could also potentially occur with wind and solar power, particularly if this expansion has very significant impacts on local and regional environments through large-scale installations of wind and solar farms and substantial extensions of the electricity grid (Cohen et al. 2014; Demski et al. 2015). It is also notable that the threat of climate change, probably due to its futurity and causal indeterminacy, has not generated the same sense of 'existential crisis' that, for example, emerged in the 1970s with the OPEC-driven oil crisis. This earlier crisis did genuinely lead to fundamental changes in global energy systems. The problem, as Giddens has noted, with the phenomenon of climate change is that by the time there is a sufficient sense of crisis, it might already be too late to avoid the damaging impacts (Giddens 2009). In the meantime, populist politicians, such as Donald Trump, gain popularity through denial of climate change and a resolve to protect the fossil fuel industries.

However, despite these potential sources of pessimism, there are more hopeful and optimistic prospective future developments. The first thing to recognize is that the neo-Malthusian projection of ever-continuing exponential growth is overly deterministic and not inevitable. This is seen, for example, in population growth where more and more countries are experiencing the so-called 'demographic transition', where societies shift from a high to a low birth and death rate and population growth stabilizes or declines (Chenais 1992). A similar phenomenon is evident also in relation to energy systems. The earlier industrial revolutions, relying on coal and oil respectively, did lead to exponential energy growth as they were 'energy-expanding' in the sense that they greatly expanded energy demand. However, the latest industrial or post-industrial revolution, which has involved a transition to expanded use of electricity and has also converged with a revolution in information and communications technology (ICT), has been in contrast 'energy-saving', resulting in a reduction in dependence on energy among the developed world since the 1970s and the stabilization of per capita energy consumption (Kander et al. 2014).

Significant further progress can be made in maximizing the gains of this shift to electricity and integration with advances in ICT. As has been noted before, many energy services currently supplied by other fuels could be electrified. The most important example of this is the potential to replace petrol and diesel with electric cars. Greater dependence on electricity is also beneficial as this is the sector which is most easily decarbonized, as is seen in the striking advances in wind and solar power. Overall, therefore, higher levels of electrification and greater use of renewables in the generation of that electricity, along with the greater energy efficiencies gained in this transition, is a realistic and, to some extent, emerging future trajectory which will have a positive impact on reducing GHG emissions. Particularly with the increase of intermittent sources of energy into the grid, the role of ICT in shifting electricity systems from being passive to active and being able to regulate supply and demand through smart technologies will be critical in ensuring the sustainability of this transition.

Another factor which can potentially make a significant and immediate difference to CO_2 emissions is to make concerted global efforts to substitute as much coal as possible with gas. As noted in the previous chapter, gas emits less than half the emissions of coal and is generally significantly cleaner and less polluting. The large-scale discovery of plentiful supplies of unconventional gas along with the potential development of a global LNG-based gas market creates the market conditions for this substitution to take place. What is required to make this a reality is the political will to support the globalization of this trade and to overcome the energy security fears that this increased global role of gas would play. For example, European countries have generally failed to capitalize as much as they could on these opportunities due to a mix of fears over the security of gas supplies, the domestic resistance to shale gas development, a tendency to prioritize renewables over 'transition' fuels such as gas, and the fact that traditional fossil fuels such as coal remain relatively cheap. However, when viewed from a global perspective, large absolute gains in reducing emissions come from even relatively small shifts of energy use from coal to gas and require considerably less effort than the full-scale transition and development of modern renewable energy sources.

A final source of optimism draws from the conclusions of the previous chapter that states are generally supporting gradual and incremental change, keeping their 'options open' through encouraging a wide diversity of old and new energy sources and technologies. This cautious incrementalism can be viewed as demonstrating a lack of seriousness in confronting the challenge of climate change. However, supporting diversity and 'putting your eggs in different baskets' can also be an effective way of promoting competition, innovation and, most importantly, accommodating otherwise irreconcilable socio-economic interests (Stirling 2010: 150–4). In reality, there are multiple differing and unpredictable ways in which a sustainable energy transition will develop as this is a highly complex and multi-faceted process. It might not be, for example, the current renewables, such as wind and solar power, which ultimately underpin the transition to a non-fossil fuel energy system and it could be revolutionary new technologies that have only barely been developed so far. For example, a fundamental breakthrough in terms of electricity storage could be radically transformative. These are best viewed as hopes rather than expectations, but investing in new technologies, something that our dependence on cheap fossil fuels has tended to lead us to under-invest in, is the only sure way of making such hopes potentially fulfilled.

Conclusion

This chapter has explored the limits of our exploitation of the bountiful fossil fuel energy resources that have made possible the extraordinary global economic expansion that has taken place over the last century and a half. In terms of the history of the planet, and even in terms of human history, this transformation has taken place in a very small period of time. But the magnitude of the transformation is truly remarkable with the human population growing from one billion in 1800 to seven billion in 2016 and with per capita income growing nine-fold in the same period despite this massive population growth. The peak oil thesis and the climate change challenge raise fundamental questions about the sustainability of such dependence on fossil fuels to generate such prospective fast growth into the future.

John McNeill has called this commitment to such exponential economic growth a 'giant gamble' we are waging with the planet (McNeill 2000: 4). We are counting on the human capacity for innovation, ingenuity and experimentation to make sure that the gamble finally pays off. The problem is not, as this chapter demonstrates, that we are likely to run out soon of the precious fossil fuels that have made possible this economic transformation. If there is a 'peak' or 'tipping point', it will be with the realization that the negative effects of climate change, mainly caused by the emissions from burning fossil fuels, are so severe that decisive and drastic action needs to be taken to make a transition from a fossil fuel-based energy system.

The chapter has demonstrated that, despite a strong coalition of forces that has made climate change one of the defining issues of our time, there has actually been very little progress in moving away from the use of fossil fuels and thus reducing CO_2 emissions. The reasons for this are not a lack of environmental awareness. The efforts expended over the global climate change regime, despite the limitations, are testament to the perceived seriousness of the issue. The problem is rather that there are competing interests and objectives which continue to take precedence over the issue of sustainability (Andrews-Speed 2016). The values of energy security and economic prosperity, particularly for developing countries seeking to make the transition to modernity, have tended to take priority over the value of sustainability. The problem is also that the issue of climate change is one of those global problems that the anarchical system of nation-states, lacking an overarching global sovereign authority, is particularly unsuited to finding a comprehensive and durable resolution to. This is because of the ways in which the costs and benefits are unequally distributed, given the differing impacts of climate change on different regions. The risks and threats are also not clearly identifiable as they will only be fully known in the future and will be dependent on the extent of the change in the global climate, which is itself dependent on what actions are taken now to address this issue. All of this leads to a classic collective action problem which is the responsibility of everyone but also of no-one in particular.

The question of how pessimistic or optimistic one should be given the enormity of the challenge ahead is inevitably speculative. There are reasons, as noted above, for both pessimism and optimism. But what is certainly unlikely to emerge is a simple, comprehensive solution to this problem; if this is to occur, it will most likely be incremental, differentiated and cumulative. The development of China's energy and environmental policies provides a good illustration of this. As has been noted earlier, a very significant factor behind the increase in emissions over the last two decades has been China's very fast economic growth, which has been fuelled primarily by the large domestic endowment of coal, though this was supplemented by coal imports as well as imports of oil and gas (Dannreuther 2011). Despite the extensive environmental damage that this has caused in China, economic development trumped environmental concerns. In its engagement with the Kyoto Protocol, China has traditionally been unwilling to set a commitment to absolute reductions in its CO_2 emissions.

However, this changed in November 2014 with a China–US Joint Announcement on Climate Change, where China set a target for the peaking of carbon dioxide emissions to occur in 2030 and with the aspiration to peak earlier. As mentioned above, 2015 was also the first year when global emissions themselves did not grow, which was primarily due to China beginning to rein in its heavy coal dependence. In the China–US announcement, China also committed itself to raise clean energy sources to 20 per cent of total primary energy by 2020. This reflects the fact, not widely appreciated, that China has built a renewable energy system, using wind, hydro and solar power, which is larger than the combined renewable systems of the United States, Germany, India and Spain (Mathews and Tan 2015: 2). It has also not done this primarily for environmental reasons, despite growing public disquiet over levels of pollution found in the country. Rather, China's renewables policy has been driven more by the belief that renewables will be a valuable industry of the future and thus worth investing in for strictly economic reasons. In addition, developing renewable energy, which uses the resources found domestically and is not dependent on foreign supplies, is also viewed as strengthening China's energy security.

It is clearly an open question whether this new strategic orientation in China will be sufficient to create a new clean energy system which will avert the damage that is being inflicted with the older carbon-intensive industries. However, it does illustrate that energy security concerns, allied with economic interests, are potentially reconcilable with concerns over sustainability even in fast developing countries.

— 8 —

Conclusion

This book has sought to capture the complex multi-dimensional nature of energy security. It has included the different levels at which energy security concerns are evident; at the individual, national and global levels. It has placed these within a historical context which highlights structural legacies and constraints but also recognizes the role of contingency and the potential for innovative change. As such, the book understands energy security as conditioned by shifting social, economic and political contexts and not as a fixed given or an unchanging objective reality. It is this dynamic and continually evolving role of energy security that has been at the heart of this book and explains its wide-ranging scope and comprehensive coverage.

Nevertheless, there are a number of cross-cutting dimensions and themes which emerge from these chapters. This concluding chapter will expand on some of these key common themes and seek to articulate more clearly their significance in advancing our understanding of energy security. Three dimensions in particular are identified: the physicality of energy resources; the legacies of history; and the role of power and justice.

The Physicality of Energy Resources

Ultimately, energy is a physical and material reality that is expressed and instantiated in differing physical and material ways. Without knowledge or recognition of this, understandings and conceptualizations of energy security will inevitably be flawed. Energy resources come in differing material forms, whether concentrated or diffuse (fossil fuels as against renewables like wind and solar), hard (coal), liquid (oil) or gaseous (natural gas). These natural resources are extracted, transported and transformed in differing ways, dependent on their specific physical and material attributes. Their impacts on the environment differ similarly dependent on specific physical factors. These resources are also located in differing parts of the world, in differing levels of concentration, and this is a physical reality that sets a critical underlying condition for defining energy security.

Energy security cannot, therefore, ignore these fundamental physical attributes and these need to be incorporated in any analysis. This is evident in the preceding chapters. As highlighted in chapter 3, the physical attributes of coal have historically led to a fundamentally different set of energy security concerns compared to oil. Nevertheless, as chapter 4 argues, oil has pride of place in energy security terms because of its concentration in some of the most unstable parts of the world and due to its higher economic rent and its efficiency and adaptability as a resource. But, as noted also in the same chapter, the supply of natural gas can in certain circumstances generate high levels of energy insecurity, such as in Europe, where reliance on intercontinental pipelines makes gas, rather than oil, a significant energy security issue between Russia and Europe.

All of this means that energy security cannot be understood as something entirely socially constructed, despite the popularity of social constructivist accounts of energy security. There is a hard physical reality that needs to be recognized and incorporated. But this recognition of the material underpinnings of energy security still leaves the question of the extent of its significance. In chapter 5, there was an extended assessment of the 'resource curse' thesis that argues that the possession and extraction of valuable natural resources, such as oil and gas, results in countries having poorer developmental results and higher levels of authoritarianism compared to non-resource-rich countries. In chapter 7, there was an analysis of the 'peak oil' thesis that identifies scarcity of supply as an immediate energy security concern. In both these arguments, it is the physical properties of key energy resources leading to certain outcomes – the 'resource curse' and 'peak oil' – that are presented as the key determinants of energy insecurity.

The conclusions of this book do not support these arguments. In the 'resource curse' case, the causal logic between possession of energy resources and poor development outcomes was taken to be too deterministic and as failing to incorporate the specificities of the socio-political conditions in resource-rich states and regions. This critique included examples of countries that have bucked the trend, enjoying a resource 'blessing' rather than a 'curse'. But the more fundamental argument was that the underlying factors contributing to cases of 'resource curse' need to take account of the particular histories of state formation and of the legacies of state–society relations and should not assume a simple causal logic linking resource wealth to economic failure and dictatorship. In the case of 'peak oil', the underlying critique is similar in substance, though in a different context. Here, the mistake is over-reliance on physical and geological factors to explain the limits and scarcity of resources without taking sufficient account of the broader social, economic and political conditions which contribute to both the defining and the overcoming of scarcity.

What these cases demonstrate is that the physical and material are inextricably part of understandings of energy security but that these physical and material aspects are enmeshed in a complex array of social, economic and political structures. The physical and social cannot be simply divorced or separated from one another. It is the particular challenge for those analysing energy security to understand this complex interaction and to be able to identify the relative contribution that these different parts play in the construction of concerns over energy security. As such, energy security is best understood as resembling a Russian doll with multiple layers where the physical, social, economic and political become interlinked in complex and differing ways.

The Legacies of History

The layers of this Russian doll image of energy security also incorporate within them historical legacies and accretions. It is a core argument of this book that the historical context and the development of energy security over time is essential for a deeper understanding of the evolving meanings of the concept. As the previous chapter argued, there are historically embedded path dependencies in our current energy systems that act as powerful obstacles and constraints to the ambition to make a transition away from our dependence on fossil fuels. The accumulated $20 trillion fossil fuel infrastructure presents a strong structural impediment to radical change. Powerful constituencies and communities, whose economic prosperity and ways of life are dependent on this infrastructure, represent political forces that directly challenge governments and states. These include mining communities, large oil and gas multinational companies and a complex variety of lobbying groups supporting the economic interests of their particular energy resource, whether coal, oil, gas or nuclear. But it also includes individual citizens who, particularly in developed but also increasingly in developing countries, see their fundamental freedoms, whether to own and drive cars, to travel cheaply by plane, or more generally to continue to enjoy the benefits of their high energy-consuming lifestyles, as threatened by a fundamental shift away from dependence on the existing fossil fuel-dominated infrastructure.

A historical perspective is also important because it is essential for understanding how the concept of energy security changes over time and place. As detailed in chapter 3, energy security had a different social, economic and political meaning when coal was the dominant global energy resource compared to the subsequent period when oil became hegemonic. In the coal era, the key concern was the domestic security challenges posed by the militancy of mining communities; in the oil era, the focus changed to the international security challenges of oil-rich post-colonial countries who sought to stand up to the Western-dominated status quo. Indeed, it was the OPEC-led challenge in the 1970s that gave a wider popular recognition of energy security as an existential challenge. The legacy of this is that the concept is still strongly tied to the intermingling of oil exports and Middle Eastern instability. However, energy security has a wider scope and, as chapter 5 demonstrated, includes an intra-state domestic security dimension. But the question of how energy resources are distributed and managed within states, and the security implications of this, also have specific historical contexts that need to be understood and incorporated into any analysis.

Energy security also benefits from being viewed from a longer historical context, taking the viewpoint of the *longue durée*. From this broader perspective, the most important historical caesura is the transition from the pre-industrial to the industrial era. In the pre-industrial era, energy security was defined by the limits of power and the structural constraints to social, economic and political development. With the advent of the industrial era, economic security was re-defined by the seemingly limitless expansion of power and the liberation from these earlier constraints to social, economic and political development. Although there are multiple factors which contributed to this historical transition, the development of the technical knowledge to be able more fully to exploit the energy-expanding potential of the earth's reserves of fossil fuels was critical. Human population has increased seven-fold and global prosperity, albeit highly unevenly distributed, has grown at an even greater rate. But the security implications of this power expansion has led, in its extreme manifestation, to the prospect of human self-destruction. Through the development of nuclear fission, mankind now has the capacity to destroy itself, and the habitats on which it depends, through nuclear warfare. In addition, through the accumulation of the atmospheric pollution generated by the use of fossil fuels, there is a real prospect of global atmospheric warming leading to widescale destruction of our natural ecosystems.

This broader perspective also contextualizes the dominant narratives of energy security and this book presents two specific contested narratives. The first narrative is the 'modernizing narrative', which highlights the benefits for human prosperity and the social and political emancipation that have been gained through the expansion of modern energy markets and systems. The emphasis here is on the benefits that are gained through embracing market forces, such as the liberalization and globalization of energy markets. From this perspective, energy insecurity results mainly from the resistance and blocking of such modernizing dynamics. As shown in chapter 7, this approach also tends to be confident that human ingenuity and technological innovation act as powerful forces that can, with the proper support, overcome challenges such as climate change.

The second alternative historical narrative is more critical. It does not challenge the historical record of the expansion of modern power and prosperity through the various energy transitions. However, it does question the equity and fairness of the resulting social, economic and political conditions and highlights the structural inequalities that have been entrenched through the process. From this perspective, the modern fossil fuel-based global economy is one that has consolidated a particular international structure that privileges the West and has conditioned the rest of the world to political subordination as well as many of the poorest to a condition of energy poverty. Within states, these inequalities are expressed through elites gaining economic and political power through their control of energy resources, which has aided the establishment of repressive and authoritarian forms of government. In contrast to the modernizing approach, there tends to be greater pessimism about the potential for collective action to be able to respond effectively to the global challenges that threaten the sustainability of our current ways of living.

Justice and Power

It is this critical narrative that this book has sought to incorporate in its analysis of energy security, while also recognizing the power and salience of the alternative modernizing narrative. This is a key reason why it is the *politics* of energy security that is the main framework for this book, basing its main theoretical foundations in security studies and the discipline of International Relations. The analytical advantage of privileging a political framework is that it draws out and highlights the critical role that considerations of power and justice play in the shifting conceptions of energy security. This is not to reduce the importance of other disciplinary insights or to deny that a comprehensive understanding of energy security demands an interdisciplinary approach. These have also been incorporated in the analysis, where appropriate. However, the particular aim of this book is to give a more distinct expression of the ideological and normative dimension of competing conceptualizations of energy security and to restore a political dimension which is at times absent from other accounts. This has meant that some of the more technical aspects of energy security have not been given as much attention, such as, for example, the role of the IEA for ensuring emergency oil storage or how grid management systems can manage intermittent renewable power sources. But this has hopefully been justified through the objective of the book to 'bring back' the politics of energy security.

Politics is essentially the study of power, how power is accumulated and distributed and how these power relations are justified, legitimated and contested. Such power relations, and the issues of justice that they raise, also develop over time and have a historical dimension, while continually evolving and adapting to new conditions and circumstances. Each of the chapters in this book has sought to bring out the significance of these issues of power and justice. In chapter 4, the international tensions and conflicts over energy as they relate to the Middle East, China and Russia were shown to be inextricably tied to an underlying resentment in these regions and countries at the perceived historical injustices and failure of the West to treat them with dignity and respect. In chapter 5, the domestic insecurities in many resource-rich countries, whether expressed through a repressive state apparatus or through the breakdown of civil order, are similarly due to the perceived societal injustices of the distribution of the benefits of these resources and the broader societal response to the failure to support the development of the whole of society.

In chapter 6, the analysis of the different energy markets for coal, oil, nuclear, gas and renewables demonstrated that there is a continual interaction and contestation between the interests of markets and the interests of states. The balance between states and markets, in particular the role of private companies, is one which incorporates both power considerations and the determination of states to ensure that markets serve the interests of the state. The justice dimension of this becomes most clearly apparent in the global negotiations over the appropriate response to the challenge of climate change, as detailed in chapter 7. At the heart of these negotiations is the fundamental question of responsibility and whether this lies with the 'historical' emitters, such as the United States and the rest of the industrialized world, or with the 'current' emitters, in particular countries like China, whose fast economic development is the most significant reason for the current surge in GHG emissions. Justice issues also have here an intergenerational dimension, where the question is whether the main costs for mitigating climate change should be borne by the current generation or can legitimately be left for future and potentially richer generations. The book concludes, therefore, with the question of how to reconcile issues of power and justice being central to the most critical challenge facing our energy futures.

Energy Security as a Value

In summary, the concept of energy security needs to include these three dimensions – the physicality of energy; the legacies of history; and considerations of power and justice. It is constant attention to these different elements that the full meaning of energy security, contextualized in time and place, can be properly understood. Energy security is difficult to define precisely because there is a continually shifting context and because it includes a normative dimension which cannot be reduced to a purely technical question. Energy security is, as argued in chapter 2, a value that cannot be treated in isolation but only in relation to, and in contestation with, other values. Energy security competes, in particular, with the values of economic prosperity and sustainability. The larger picture is what Aristotle calls the 'good life' – energy security contributes to the goal but only if it can also promote social and economic development for all and ensure that our civilization is environmentally sustainable. It can also do this when it is embedded in global and national power structures that are mutually recognized to be just and legitimate. Energy security is, thus, ultimately a political project and a critically important one for ensuring a 'good life' for all. It is this which makes the subject of energy security both fascinating and urgent.

References

Aalto, P. (ed.) (2016) *The EU-Russian Energy Dialogue: Europe's Future Energy Security*, London: Routledge.

Adelman, M. A. (2004) 'The real oil problem', *Regulation*, 27(1): 16–21.

Africa Progress Panel (2013) 'Equity in extractives: stewarding Africa's natural resources for all'. Available at: http://app-cdn.acwupload.co.uk/wp-content/uploads/2013/08/2013_APR_Equity_in_Extractives_25062013_ENG_HR.pdf

Aissaoui, A. (2001) *Algeria: The Political Economy of Oil and Gas*, Oxford: Oxford University Press.

Al-Sowayegh, A. (1984) *Arab Petropolitics*, London: Croom Helm.

Alexeev, M. and R. Conrad (2009) 'The elusive curse of oil', *Review of Economics and Statistics*, 91(3): 586–98.

Anderson, K. (2015) 'Duality in climate science', *Nature Geoscience*, 8: 898–900.

Anderson, L. (1987) 'The state in the Middle East and North Africa', *Comparative Politics*, 20(1): 1–18.

Andrews-Speed, P. (2016) 'Applying institutional theory to the low-carbon transition', *Energy Research and Social Science*, 13: 216–25.

Andrews-Speed, P. and R. Dannreuther (2011) *China, Oil and Global Politics*, London: Routledge.

Andrews-Speed, P., R. Bleischwitz, T. Boersma, C. Johnson, G. Kemp and S. D. VanDeveer (2012) *The Global Resource*

Nexus: The Struggles for Land, Energy, Food, Water and Minerals, Washington, DC: Transatlantic Academy.

Antes, R., B. Hansjuergens, P. Letmathe and S. Pickl (eds) (2011) *Emissions Trading: Institutional Design, Decision Making and Corporate Strategies*, Dordrecht: Springer.

Arrighi, G. and B. Silver (1984) 'Labor movements and capital migration: the US and Western Europe in world-historical perspective', in C. Bergquist (ed.) *Labor in the Capitalist World-Economy*, Beverly Hills, CA: Sage, pp. 183–216.

Arthur, B. (1994) *Increasing Returns and Path Dependence in the Economy*, Ann Arbor, MI: University of Michigan Press.

Auty, R. M. (1994) 'Industrial policy reform in six large newly industrializing countries: the resource curse thesis', *World Development*, 22(1): 11–26.

Auty, R. M. (2001) 'The political economy of resource-driven growth', *European Economic Review*, 45: 839–46.

Baev, P. K. (2007) 'Russia aspires to the status of "energy superpower"', *Strategic Analysis*, 31(3): 447–65.

Bailey, R. (2013) 'The "food versus fuel" nexus', in A. Goldthau (ed.) *The Handbook of Global Energy Policy*, Chichester: Wiley-Blackwell, pp. 265–81.

Bairoch, P. (1983) 'Energie et révolution industrielle: nouvelles perspectives', *Revue de l'energie*, 356: 399–408.

Baldwin, D. A. (1997) 'The concept of security', *Review of International Studies*, 23(1): 5–26.

Ball, J. (2012) 'Tough love for renewable energy', *Foreign Affairs*, 91(3): 122–33.

Ballentine, K. and J. Sherman (eds) (2003) *The Political Economy of Armed Conflict: Beyond Greed and Grievance*, Boulder, CO: Lynne Rienner.

Baran, P. (1957) *The Political Economy of Growth*, New York: Monthly Review Press.

Baran, P. and P. Sweezy (1966) *Monopoly Capitalism*, New York: Monthly Review Press.

Baumann, F. (2008) 'Energy security as a multidimensional concept', Centre for Applied Policy Research: *Policy Analysis*, No. 1. Available at: http://www.cap.lmu.de/download/2008/CAP-Policy-Analysis-2008-01.pdf

Beblawi, H. (1987) 'The rentier state in the Arab world', in H. Beblawi and G. Luciani (eds) *The Rentier State: Volume II*, London: Croom Helm, pp. 49–62.

Belyi, A. V. (2015) *Transnational Gas Markets and Euro-Russian Energy Relations*, Basingstoke: Palgrave.

Belyi, A. V. and K. Talus (2015) *States and Markets in Hydrocarbon Sectors*, Basingstoke: Palgrave.

Benedick, R. (1998) *Ozone Diplomacy: New Directions in Safeguarding the Planet*, Cambridge, MA: Harvard University Press.

Bhattacharyya, S. (2013) 'Energy access and development', in A. Goldthau (ed.) *The Handbook of Global Energy Policy*, Chichester: Wiley-Blackwell, pp. 227–43.

Blank, S. (1995) 'Energy, economics and security in Central Asia: Russia and its rivals', *Central Asian Survey*, 14(3): 373–406.

Boccard, N. (2014) 'The cost of nuclear electricity: France after Fukushima', *Energy Policy*, 66: 450–61.

Booth, A. (1995) 'The state and the economy in Indonesia in the nineteenth and twentieth century', in J. Harris, J. Hunter and C. M. Lewis (eds) *The New Institutional Economics and Third World*, London: Routledge, pp. 283–305.

Boserup, E. (1965) *The Conditions of Agricultural Growth*, London: Earthscan.

Bradshaw, M. J. (2009) 'The geopolitics of global energy security', *Geography Compass*, 3(5): 1920–37.

Bradshaw, M. J. (2014) *Global Energy Dilemmas*, Cambridge: Polity.

Brautigam, D. (2009) *The Dragon's Gift: the Real Story of China in Africa*, Oxford: Oxford University Press.

Bremmer, I. (2008) 'The return of state capitalism', *Survival*, 50(3): 55–64.

Bremmer, I. (2009) 'State capitalism comes of age: the end of the free market?', *Foreign Affairs*, 88(3): 40–55.

Bremmer, I. and R. Johnston (2009) 'The rise and fall of resource nationalism', *Survival*, 51(2): 149–58.

Bressand, A. (2012) 'The changing geopolitics of energy and climate change and the challenge for Europe', CIEP Papers, no. 4. Available at: http://www.clingendaelenergy.com/inc/upload/files/The_changed_geopolitics_of_energy_and_climate_bressand.pdf

Bressand, A. (2013) 'The role of markets and investment in global energy', in A. Goldthau (ed.) *The Handbook of Global Energy Policy*, Chichester: Wiley-Blackwell, pp. 15–29.

Bridge, G. (2008) 'Global production networks and the extractive sector: governing resource-based development', *Journal of Economic Geography*, 8(3): 389–419.

Bridge, G. (2010) 'Past peak oil: political economy of energy crises', in R. Peet, P. Robbins and M. Watts (eds) *Global Political Ecology*, London: Routledge, pp. 307–24.

Bridge, G. and P. Le Billon (2013) *Oil*, Cambridge: Polity.

British Petroleum (2014) *Statistical Review of World Energy*, London: British Petroleum.

Bromley, S. (2005) 'The United States and control of world oil', *Government and Opposition*, 40(2): 225–55.

Brown, L. C. (1984) *International Politics of the Middle East: Old Rules, Dangerous Games*, Princeton, NJ: Princeton University Press.

Buzan, B. (1999) 'Rethinking security after the Cold War', *Cooperation and Conflict*, 32(1): 5–28.

Buzan, B., O. Waever and J. de Wilde (1998) *Security: A New Framework of Analysis*, Boulder, CO: Lynne Rienner.

Callinicos, A. (2005) 'Iraq: fulcrum of world politics', *Third World Quarterly*, 26(4/5): 593–608.

Camp, M. (2014) 'Carter's energy insecurity: the political economy of coal in the 1970s', *Journal of Policy History*, 26(4): 459–78.

Campbell, C. and J. Laherrere (1998) 'The end of cheap oil?', *Scientific American*, 278(3): 78–84.

Canning, K. (1996) *Languages of Labour and Gender: Female Factory Work in Germany, 1850–1911*, Ithaca, NY: Cornell University Press.

Chen, M. E. and A. M. Jaffe (2007) 'Energy security and national oil companies', *The Whitehead Journal of Diplomacy and International Relations*, 8(1): 9–21.

Chenais, J. C. (1992) *The Demographic Transition: Stages, Patterns and Economic Implications*, Oxford: Oxford University Press.

Cherp, A. and J. Jewell (2011) 'The three perspectives on energy security: intellectual history, the disciplinary roots and the potential for integration', *Current Opinion in Environmental Sustainability*, 3: 1–11.

Chester, L. (2010) 'Conceptualizing energy security and making explicit its polysemic nature', *Energy Policy*, 55(2): 887–95.

Church, R. A., Q. Outram and D. N. Smith (1991) 'The militancy of British miners, 1893–1986: interdisciplinary problems and perspectives', *Journal of Interdisciplinary History*, 22(1): 49–66.

Churchill, R. S. (1968) *Winston Churchill: Young Statesman, 1901–1914*, London: Heinemann.

Cipolla, C. M. (1962) *The Economic History of World Population*, Harmondsworth: Penguin.

Clark, P. (2015) 'Carbon capture: miracle machine or white elephant?', *Financial Times*, 9 September. Available at: http://www.ft.com/cms/s/2/88c187b4-5619-11e5-a28b-50226830d644.html#axzz4IoFoRRZV

Cohen, J. J., J. Reichl and M. Schmidthaler (2014) 'Re-focussing research efforts on the public acceptance of energy infrastructure: a critical review', *Energy*, 76: 4–9.

Cole, P. and B. McQuinn (eds) (2015) *The Libyan Revolution and its Aftermath*, Oxford: Oxford University Press.

Colgan, J. D. (2012) 'Oil and revolutionary governments: fuel for international conflicts', *International Organization*, 99(1): 24–39.

Collier, P. (2008) *The Bottom Billion*, Oxford: Oxford University Press.

Collier, P. and A. Hoeffler (2002) 'On the incidence of civil war in Africa', *Journal of Conflict Resolution*, 46(1): 13–28.

Collier, P. and A. Hoeffler (2004) 'Greed and grievance in civil war', *Oxford Economic Papers*, 56: 563–95.

Collier, P., A. Hoeffler, H. Hegre, M. Reyna-Quirol and N. Sambanis (2003) *Breaking the Conflict Trap*, Washington, DC: World Bank and Oxford University Press.

Commission on Human Security (2003) *Human Security Now: Protecting and Empowering People*, New York: Commission on Human Security.

Cornot-Gandolphe, S. (2014) *China's Coal Market: Can Beijing Tame 'King Coal'*, Oxford: Oxford Institute for Energy Studies.

Cox, E., P. Johnstone and A. Stirling (2016) 'Understanding the intensity of UK policy commitments to nuclear power', *SPRU Working Papers*, September. Available at: https://www.sussex.ac.uk/webteam/gateway/file.php?name=2016-16-swps-cox-et-al.pdf&site=25

Cox, R. W. (1981) 'Social forces, states and world orders: beyond international relations theory', *Millennium*, 10(2): 126–55.

Cragg, C. (2013) 'History of the gas industry', in R. Dannreuther and W. Ostrowski (eds) *Global Resources: Conflict and Cooperation*, Basingstoke: Palgrave Macmillan, pp. 59–76.

Criqui, P. (2013) 'Peak oil: myth or impending doom', in R. Dannreuther and W. Ostrowski (eds) *Global Resources: Conflict and Cooperation*, Basingstoke: Palgrave Macmillan, pp. 187–205.

Crosby, A. W. (2006) *Children of the Sun: A History of Humanity's Unappeasable Appetite for Energy*, New York: W. W. Norton.

Cumings, B. (1987) 'The origins and development of the Northeast Asian political economy', in F. Deyo (ed.) *The Political Economy of the New Asian Industrialism*, Ithaca, NY: Cornell University Press, pp. 44–83.

Dannreuther, R. (1992) *The Gulf War: A Political and Strategic Analysis*, London: Brassey's for the International Institute for Strategic Studies.

Dannreuther, R. (2011) 'China and global oil', *International Affairs*, 87(6): 1345–64.

Dannreuther, R. (2013) *International Security: the Contemporary Agenda*, Cambridge: Polity.

Dannreuther, R. and W. Ostrowski (eds) (2013) *Global Resources: Conflict and Cooperation*, Basingstoke: Palgrave Macmillan.

David, P. A. (1985) 'Clio and the economics of QWERTY', *American Economic Review*, 75: 332–7.

David, P. A. and G. Wright (1997) 'Increasing returns and the genesis of American resource abundance', *Industrial and Corporate Change*, 6(2): 203–45.

de Soysa, I. (2002) 'Paradise is a bazaar? Greed, creed and governance in civil war, 1989–99', *Journal of Peace Research*, 39(4): 395–416.

Deffeyes, K. (2001) *Hubbert's Peak: The Impending World Oil Shortage*, Princeton, NJ: Princeton University Press.

Demski, C., C. Butler, K. A. Parkhill, A. Spence and N. F. Pidgeon (2015) 'Public values for energy systems change', *Global Environmental Change*, 34: 56–61.

Depledge, J. (2015) 'The global climate change regime', in P. Ekins, M. Bradshaw and J. Watson (eds) *Global Energy: Issues, Potentials, and Policy Implications*, Oxford: Oxford University Press, pp. 73–91.

Dickel, R., E. Hassanzadeh, J. Henderson, A. Honoré, L. El-Katiri, S. Pirani, H. Rogers, J. Stern and K. Yafimara (2014) *Reducing European Dependence on Russian Gas: Distinguishing Natural Gas Security from Geopolitics*, Oxford: Oxford Institute for Energy Studies. Available at: https://www.oxfordenergy.org/wpcms/wp-content/uploads/2014/10/NG-92.pdf

Dietsche, E. (2013) 'Sector legal frameworks and resource property rights', in R. Dannreuther and W. Ostrowski (eds) *Global Resources: Conflict and Cooperation*, Basingstoke: Palgrave Macmillan, pp. 159–84.

Dodds, P. E. and B. Fais (2015) 'Network infrastructure and energy storage for low-carbon energy systems', in P. Ekins, M. Bradshaw and J. Watson (eds) *Global Energy: Issues, Potentials and Policy Implications*, Oxford: Oxford University Press, pp. 426–51.

Dodge, T. (2014) *Iraq's Future: the Aftermath of Regime Change*, London: Routledge for the International Institute for Strategic Studies.

Dorrien, G. (2004) *Imperial Dangers: Neoconservatives and the new Pax Americana*, London: Routledge.

Dos Santos, T. (1969) 'The crisis of development theory and the problem of dependence in Latin America', in H. Berstein (ed.) *Underdevelopment and Development*, London: Penguin, pp. 57–80.

Downs, E. S. (2004) 'The Chinese energy security debate', *China Quarterly*, 177: 21–41.

Downs, E. S. (2007) 'The fact and fiction in Sino-African energy relations', *China Security*, 3(3): 42–68.

Duchâtel, M. and F. Godement (2016) 'China and Russia: Gaming the West', *China Analysis*. Available at: http://www.ecfr.eu/page/-/ECFR_195_-_CHINA_AND_RUSSIA_GAMING_THE_WEST_(002).pdf

Dunning, T. (2005) 'Resource dependence, economic performance and political stability', *Journal of Conflict Resolution*, 49(4): 451–82.

Economist (2012) 'Special report: nuclear energy: the dream that failed', *Economist*, 11 March.

Eide, A. (2008) *The Right to Food and the Impact of Liquid Biofuels (Agrofuels)*, Rome: Food and Agriculture Organization.

Ekins, P., M. Bradshaw and J. Watson (eds) (2015) *Global Energy: Issues, Potentials, and Policy Implications*, Oxford: Oxford University Press.

Eley, G. (2002) *Forging Democracy: The History of the Left in Europe, 1850–2000*, Oxford: Oxford University Press.

Elkind, J. (2010) 'Energy security: call for a broader agenda', in C. Pascual and J. Elkind (eds) *Energy Security: Economics, Politics, Strategies and Implications*, Washington, DC: Brookings Institution Press, pp. 119–48.

Elliot, D. (2013) *Fukushima: Impacts and Implications*, Basingstoke: Palgrave Macmillan.

Elliot, L. (2006) 'Cosmopolitan environmental harm conventions', *Global Society*, 20(3): 346–63.

Ericsson, M. and P. Soderholm (2013) 'Minerals depletion and peak production', in R. Dannreuther and W. Ostrowski (eds) *Global Resources: Conflict and Cooperation*, Basingstoke: Palgrave Macmillan, pp. 222–31.

Fardmanesh, M. (1991) 'Dutch disease economics and the oil syndrome: an empirical study', *World Politics*, 19(6): 711–17.

Fearon, J. D. and D. D. Laitin (2002) 'Ethnicity, insurgency and civil war', *American Political Science Review*, 97(1): 75–90.

Ferdinand, P. (2007) 'Russia and China: converging responses to globalization', *International Affairs*, 83(4): 655–80.

Finlay, L., H. Jeffery, A. MacGillivray and G. Aggidis (2015) 'Water; ocean energy and hydro', in P. Ekins, M. Bradshaw and J. Watson (eds) *Global Energy: Issues, Potentials and Policy Implications*, Oxford: Oxford University Press, pp. 377–403.

Fitzgerald, J. (2012) 'The messy politics of "clean coal": the shaping of a contested term in Appalachia's energy debate', *Organization and Environment*, 25(4): 437–51.

Franke, A., A. Gawrich and G. Alakhbarov (2009) 'Kazakhstan and Azerbaijan as post-rentier states: resource incomes and autarchy as a double "curse" in post-Soviet regimes', *Europe-Asia Studies*, 61(2): 109–40.

Freedman, L. and E. Karsh (1994) *The Gulf Conflict, 1990–1991: Diplomacy and War in the New World Order*, London: Faber and Faber.

Freese, B. (2003) *Coal: A Human History*, London: Arrow Books.

Friedberg, A. L. (2005) 'The future of US–China relations: is conflict inevitable?', *International Security*, 30(2): 7–45.

Friedman, T. L. (2006) 'The first law of petropolitics', *Foreign Policy*, 154: 28–39.

Frynas, J. G. and M. Paulo (2007) 'A new scramble for African oil? Historical, political and business perspectives', *African Affairs*, 106(423): 229–51.

Fukuyama, F. (1992) *The End of History and the Last of Man*, London: Hamish Hamilton.

Furtado, C. (1970) *Obstacles to Development in Latin America*, New York: Anchor Books.

Gellner, E. (1990) *Plough, Sword and Book: The Structure of Human History*, Chicago, IL: University of Chicago Press.

Gerges, F. (2005) *The Far Enemy: Why Jihad Went Global*, Cambridge: Cambridge University Press.

Gerges, F. (2016) *A History of ISIS*, Princeton, NJ: Princeton University Press.

Giddens, A. (2009) *The Politics of Climate Change*, Cambridge: Polity.

Goldberg, S. and R. Rosner (2011) *Nuclear Reactors: Generation to Generation*, Cambridge, MA: American Academy of Arts and Sciences.

Goldemberg, J., T. Johannsson, A. K. N. Reddy and R. Williams (1988) *Energy for a Sustainable World*, New Delhi: Wiley Eastern.

Goldman, M. (2008) *Oilopoly: Putin, Power and the Rise of the New Russia*, Oxford: Oneworld Publications.

Goldthau, A. (ed.) (2013) *The Handbook of Global Energy Policy*, Chichester: Wiley-Blackwell.

Goldthau, A. and N. Sitter (2015) *A Liberal Actor in a Realist World: The European Union Regulatory State and the Global Political Economy of Energy*, Cambridge: Cambridge University Press.

Goldthau, A. and J. M. Witte (2009a) 'Back to the future or forward to the past? Strengthening markets and rules for effective global energy governance', *International Affairs*, 85(2): 373–90.

Goldthau, A. and J. M. Witte (eds) (2009b) *Global Energy Governance: the New Rules of the Game*, Washington, DC: Brookings Institution.

Goodrich, C. (1925) *The Miner's Freedom: A Study of the Working Life in a Changing Industry*, Boston, MA: Marshall Jones.

Gowing, M. and L. Arnold (1974) *Independence and Deterrence: Britain and Atomic Energy, 1945–1952*, London: Macmillan.

Graulau, J. (2008) 'Is mining good for development? The intellectual history of an unresolved question', *Progress in Development Studies*, 8(2): 129–62.

Grieco, J. (1988) 'Anarchy and the limits of cooperation: a realist critique of the newest liberal institutionalism', *International Organization*, 42(3): 488–507.

Gunton, T. (2003) 'Natural resources and regional development: an assessment of dependency and comparative advantage paradigms', *Economic Geography*, 79(1): 67–94.

Gustafson, T. (2012) *Wheel of Fortune: The Battle for Oil and Power in Russia*, Cambridge, MA: Belknap Press.

Haas, P. M. (1990) 'Obtaining international environmental protection through epistemic communities', *Millennium*, 19(3): 347–64.

Haber, S. and V. Menaldo (2011) 'Do natural resources fuel authoritarianism? A reappraisal of the resource curse', *American Political Science Review*, 105(1): 1–26.

Hamm, G. and A. Borison (2008) 'The rush to coal: is the analysis complete?', *Electricity Journal*, 21(1): 31–7.

Hartley, K. and T. Sandler (1999) 'NATO burden-sharing: past and future', *Journal of Peace Research*, 36(6): 665–80.

Harvey, D. (2003) *The New Imperialism*, Oxford: Oxford University Press.

Headrick, D. (1981) *The Tools of Empire*, Oxford: Oxford University Press.

Hecht, G. (2009) *The Radiance of France: Nuclear Power and National Identity after World War II*, Cambridge, MA: MIT Press.

Helm, D. (2012) *The Carbon Crunch: How We're Getting Climate Change Wrong – and How to Fix it*, New Haven, CT: Yale University Press.

Herring, H. (2007) 'Opposition to nuclear power: a brief history', in D. Elliot (ed.) *Nuclear or Not? Does Nuclear Power have a Place in a Sustainable Future?*, Basingstoke: Palgrave Macmillan, pp. 34–49.

Hinnebusch, R. (2003) *The International Politics of the Middle East*, Manchester: Manchester University Press.

Hinnebusch, R. (2006) 'Authoritarian persistence, democratization theory and the Middle East: an overview and critique', *Democratization*, 13(3): 373–95.

Hirschman, A. O. (1958) *The Strategy of Economic Development*, New Haven, CT: Yale University Press.

Hogselius, P. (2013) *Red Gas: Russia and the Origins of European Energy Dependence*, Basingstoke: Palgrave Macmillan.

Hojman, D. E. (2002) 'The political economy of Chile's fast growth: an Olsonian interpretation', *Public Choice*, 111: 155–78.

Homer-Dixon, T. F. (2001) *Environment, Scarcity and Violence*, Princeton, NJ: Princeton University Press.

Homer-Dixon, T. F. and J. Blitt (eds) (1998) *Ecoviolence: Links among Environment, Population, and Security*, Lanham, MD: Rowman & Littlefield.

Hopkins, R. (2014) *The Transition Handbook: From Oil Dependence to Local Resilience*, Cambridge: UIT Cambridge.

Houser, T. (2008) 'The roots of Chinese investment abroad', *Asia Policy*, 5: 141–66.

Huber, M. (2008) 'Energizing historical materialism: fossil fuels, space and the capitalist mode of production', *Geoforum*, 40: 105–15.

Hughes, T. (1983) *Networks of Power: Electrification in Western Society, 1880–1930*, Baltimore, MD: Johns Hopkins University Press.

Hulbert, M. and A. Goldthau (2013) 'Natural gas going global? Potential and pitfalls', in A. Goldthau (ed.) *The Handbook of Global Energy Policy*, Chichester: Wiley-Blackwell, pp. 98–112.

Hulme, M. (2009) *Why we Disagree about Climate Change*, Cambridge: Cambridge University Press.

Hultman, N. and J. Koomey (2013) 'Three Mile Island: the driver of US power's decline?', *Bulletin of the Atomic Scientists*, 69(3): 63–70.

Humphreys, M., J. D. Sachs and J. E. Stiglitz (2007) 'What is the problem with natural resource wealth?', in M. Humphreys,

J. D. Sachs and J. E. Stiglitz (eds) *Escaping the Resource Curse*, New York: Columbia University Press.

Huntington, S. P. (1991) *The Third Wave: Democratization in the Late Twentieth Century*, Norman, OK: University of Oklahoma Press.

Huysmans, J. (2000) 'The European Union and the securitization of migration', *Journal of Common Market Studies*, 38(5): 751–77.

IEA (2011) *Are We Entering the Golden Age of Gas*, Paris: International Energy Agency.

IEA (2015) *Key Renewables Trends*, Paris: International Energy Agency.

IEA (2016) *20 Years of Carbon Capture and Storage: Accelerating Future Development*, Paris: International Energy Agency.

Ikenberry, G. J. (2001) *After Victory: Institutions, Strategic Restraint and the Rebuilding of Order after Major Wars*, Princeton, NJ: Princeton University Press.

Ikenberry, G. J. (2012) *The Liberal Leviathan: The Origins, Crisis, and Transformation of American World Order*, Princeton, NJ: Princeton University Press.

Innis, H. (1956) *Essays in Canadian Economic History*, Toronto: Toronto University Press.

Jackson, R. B., J. G. Canadell, C. Le Quéré, R. M. Andrew, J. I. Korsbakken, G. P. Peters and N. Nakicenovica (2016) 'Reaching peak emissions', *Nature Climate Change*, 6: 7–10.

Jacobson, M. Z. and M. A. Delucchi (2011) 'Providing all global energy with wind, water and solar power: Part 1: Technologies, global resources, quantities and areas of infrastructure', *Energy Policy*, 39: 1154–69.

Jaffe, A. M. and R. A. Manning (2000) 'The shocks of a world of cheap oil', *Foreign Affairs*, 79(1): 16–29.

Jevons, W. S. (2008 [1865]) *The Coal Question: An Inquiry Concerning the Progress of the Nation, and the Probable Exhaustion of our Coal-mines*, London: Dodo Press.

Kander, A., P. Malinima and P. Warde (2014) *Power to the People: Energy in Europe over the Last Five Centuries*, Princeton, NJ: Princeton University Press.

Kaplan, R. D. (2009) 'Center stage for the 21st century: rivalry in the Indian Ocean', *Foreign Affairs*, 88(2): 16–32.

Karasac, H. (2002) 'Actors of the new "great game": Caspian oil politics', *Journal of Southern Europe and the Balkans*, 4(1): 15–27.

Karl, T. L. (1997) *The Paradox of Plenty: Oil Booms and Petro-States*, Berkeley, CA: California University Press.

Keohane, R. O. and J. Nye (1977) *Power and Interdependence: World Politics in Transition*, Boston, MA: Little, Brown.

Keohane, R. O. and D. G. Victor (2013) 'The transnational politics of energy', *Daedalus, the Journal of the American Academy of Arts and Sciences*, 142(1): 97–109.

Kessler, G. (2005) 'US says China must address its intentions: how its power is used is of concern', *Washington Post*, 22 September. Available at: http://www.washingtonpost.com/wp-dyn/content/article/2005/09/21/AR2005092101912.html

Kissinger, H. (1982) *Years of Upheaval*, New York: Weidenfeld and Nicolson.

Klare, M. T. (2001) *Resource Wars: The New Landscape of Global Conflict*, New York: Henry Holt.

Klare, M. T. (2004) *Blood and Oil: the Dangers of America's Growing Dependency on Imported Petroleum*, New York: Metropolitan Books.

Klare, M. T. (2008) *Rising Powers, Shrinking Planets: How Scarce Energy is Creating a New World Order*, Oxford: Oneworld.

Korooshy, J., A. Ibbotson, B. Lee, D. R. Bingham and W. Simons (2015) 'The low carbon economy', *Equity Research*, Goldman Sachs, 30 November. Available at: http://www.goldmansachs.com/our-thinking/pages/new-energy-landscape-folder/report-the-low-carbon-economy/report.pdf

Krasner, S. D. (ed.) (1983) *International Regimes*, Ithaca, NY: Cornell University Press.

Kryshtanovskaya, O. and S. White (2009) 'The sovietization of Russian politics', *Post-Soviet Affairs*, 25(4): 283–309.

Kuzemko, C. (2014) 'Ideas, power and change: explaining EU–Russian energy relations', *Journal of European Public Policy*, 21(1): 58–75.

Kuzemko, C., M. F. Keating and A. Goldthau (2016) *The Global Energy Challenge: Environment, Development and Security*, Basingstoke: Palgrave Macmillan.

LaBelle, M. and M. Horwitch (2013) 'The break-out of energy innovation: accelerating to a new low carbon energy system', in A. Goldthau (ed.) *The Handbook of Global Energy Policy*, Chichester: Wiley, pp. 113–26.

Landsberg, H. H. (1987) 'Rethinking energy security: the case for coal in the United States', *Environment: Science and Policy for a Sustainable Future*, 29(6): 18–43.

Lanteigne, M. (2008) 'China's maritime security and the "Malacca dilemma"', *Asian Studies*, 4(2): 143–61.

Laruelle, M. and S. Peyrouse (2009) *China as Neighbour: Central Asian Perspectives and Strategies*, Washington, DC: Johns Hopkins University Press-SAIS.

Le Billon, P. (2001) 'The political ecology of war: natural resources and armed conflicts', *Political Geography*, 20: 561–84.

Levy, M. A. (1995) 'Is the environment a national security issue?', *International Security*, 20(2): 35–62.

Lieber, R. J. (1992) 'Oil and power after the Gulf War', *International Security*, 17(1): 155–76.

Litwak, R. S. (2000) *Rogue States and US Foreign Policy: Containment after the Cold War*, Washington, DC: Woodrow Wilson Center.

Lo, B. (2008) *Axis of Convenience: Moscow, Beijing and the New Geopolitics*, Washington, DC: Brookings Institution Press.

Locatelli, C. and S. Rossiaud (2011) 'A neoinstitutionalist interpretation of the changes in the Russian oil model', *Energy Policy*, 39(9): 5588–97.

Lomborg, B. (ed.) (2004) *Global Crises, Global Solutions*, Cambridge: Cambridge University Press.

Luciani, G. (1987) 'Allocation vs. production states: a theoretical framework', in H. Beblawi and G. Luciani (eds) *The Rentier State: Volume II*, London: Croom Helm.

Luciani, G. (2011) 'Price and revenue volatility: what policy options and role for the state?', *Global Governance*, 17(2): 213–28.

Luciani, G. (2013) 'Corporations vs. states in the shaping of global oil regimes', in R. Dannreuther and W. Ostrowski (eds) *Global Resources: Conflict and Cooperation*, Basingstoke: Palgrave Macmillan, pp. 119–39.

Luft, G., A. Korin and E. Gupta (2010) 'Energy security and climate change: a tenuous link', in B. K. Sovacool (ed.) *The*

Routledge Handbook of Energy Security, London: Routledge, pp. 43–55.

Luong, P. J. and E. Weinthal (2010) *Oil is Not a Curse: Ownership Structure and Institutions in Soviet Successor States*, Cambridge: Cambridge University Press.

Lynch, M. C. (ed.) (1996) *The Analysis and Forecasting of Petroleum Supply: Sources of Error or Bias*, Boulder, CO: International Research Center for Energy and Economic Development.

Lynch, M. C. (2003) 'The new pessimism about petroleum resources: debunking the Hubbert Model (and Hubbert modelers)', *Minerals and Energy*, 18(1): 21–32.

Mackintosh, W. (1964) *The Economic Background of Dominion-Provincial Relations*, Toronto: McClelland and Stewart.

Mahbubani, K. (2008) *The New Asian Hemisphere: The Irresistible Shift of Global Power to the East*, New York: PublicAffairs.

Mahdavy, H. (1970) 'The patterns and problems of economic development in rentier states: the case of Iran', in M. A. Cook (ed.) *Studies in the Economic History of the Middle East*, Oxford: Oxford University Press, pp. 428–67.

Makiya, K. (1998) *The Republic of Fear*, Berkeley, CA: University of California Press.

Maloney, W. F. (2002) 'Innovation and growth in resource-rich countries', Central Bank of Chile Working Paper, 148. Available at: http://si2.bcentral.cl/public/pdf/documentos-trabajo/pdf/dtbc148.pdf

Malthus, R. (2003 [1820]) *An Essay on the Principle of Population*, New York: W. W. Norton.

Mann, M. (1993) *The Sources of Social Power: Volume 1: A History of Power from the Beginning to AD 1760*, Cambridge: Cambridge University Press.

Marcel, V. (2006) *Oil Titans: National Oil Companies in the Middle East*, London: Royal Institute of International Affairs.

Marks, R. B. (2002) *The Origins of the Modern World: A Global and Ecological Narrative*, Lanham, MD: Rowman and Littlefield.

Martin, R. (2015) *Coal Wars: The Future of Energy and the Future of the Planet*, Basingstoke: Macmillan.

Massachusetts Institute of Technology (2010) *The Future of Natural Gas: An Interdisciplinary Study*, Cambridge, MA: MIT Press.

Mathews, J. A. and H. Tan (2015) *China's Renewable Energy Revolution*, Basingstoke: Palgrave Macmillan.

Mathews, J. T. (1989) 'Redefining security', *Foreign Affairs*, 62(2): 162–77.

McGlade, C. and P. Ekins (2015) 'The geographical distribution of fossil fuels unused when limiting global warming to 2°C', *Nature*, 517: 187–90.

McNeill, J. R. (2000) *Something New Under the Sun: An Environmental History of the Twentieth Century*, New York: Norton.

Meadows, D. A., D. L. Meadows, J. Randers and W. H. Behrens (1972) *Beyond the Limits: Confronting Global Collapse, Envisioning a Sustainable Future*, New York: Universe Books.

Mikesell, R. (1997) 'Explaining the resource curse, with special reference to mineral-exporting countries', *Resources Policy*, 23(4): 191–9.

Miller, C. A. and P. N. Edwards (eds) (2001) *Changing the Atmosphere: Expert Knowledge and Environmental Governance*, Cambridge, MA: MIT Press.

Mitchell, T. (2009) 'Carbon democracy', *Economy and Society*, 38(3): 399–432.

Mitchell, T. (2011) *Carbon Democracy: Political Power in the Age of Oil*, London: Verso.

Montgomery, S. (2010) *The Powers That Be: Global Energy for the Twenty-First Century and Beyond*, Chicago, IL: Chicago University Press.

Moran, T. H. (1998) *Foreign Direct Investment and Development: The New Policy Agenda for Developing Countries and Economies in Transition*, Washington, DC: Institute for International Economics.

Moreira, S. (2013) 'Learning from failure: China's overseas oil investments', *Journal of Current Chinese Affairs*, 42(1): 131–65.

Moriarty, P. and D. Honnery (2016) 'Can renewable energy power the future?', *Energy Policy*, 93: 3–7.

Morse, E. L. (1999) 'A new political economy of oil?', *Journal of International Affairs*, 53(1): 1–29.

Myers, N. (1993) *Ultimate Security: the Environmental Basis of Political Stability*, New York: W. W. Norton.

Nakov, A. and G. Nuno (2013) 'Saudi Arabia and the oil market', *The Economic Journal*, 123(573): 1333–62.

National Diet of Japan (2012) *Report of the National Diet of Japan: Fukushima Nuclear Accident Independent Investigation Commission*, Tokyo: National Diet of Japan.

Newell, R. G., W. A. Pizer and D. Raimi (2013) 'Carbon markets 15 years after Kyoto: lessons learned, new challenges', *Journal of Economic Perspectives*, 27(1): 123–46.

Newnham, R. (2011) 'Oil, sticks and carrots: Russia's energy resources as a foreign policy tool', *Journal of Eurasian Studies*, 2(2): 134–43.

Nordhaus, T. and M. Shellenberger (2010) 'The end of magical climate thinking', *Foreign Affairs*, 13(1): 19–28.

Nye, D. (2010) *When the Lights Went Out*, Cambridge, MA: MIT Press.

Odell, P. (2010) 'Why we do not have to worry about peak oil', *European Energy Review*, 15 January. Available at: https://www.elektormagazine.com/news/Why-we-do-not-have-to-worry-about--peak-oil-

Okruhlik, G. (1999) 'Rentier wealth, unruly law, and the rise of opposition: the political economy of oil states', *Comparative Politics*, 31(3): 295–315.

Olson, M. (1965) *The Logic of Collective Action*, Cambridge, MA: Harvard University Press.

Olson, M. (1993) 'Dictatorship, democracy and development', *American Political Science Review*, 87(3): 567–76.

Olson, M. and R. Zeckhauser (1966) 'An economic theory of alliances', *Review of Economics and Statistics*, 48: 266–79.

Orttung, R. W. and I. Overland (2011) 'A limited toolbox: explaining the constraints on Russia's foreign energy policy', *Journal of Eurasian Studies*, 2(1): 74–85.

Ostrowski, W. (2013) 'The political economy of global resources', in R. Dannreuther and W. Ostrowski (eds) *Global Resources: Conflict and Cooperation*, Basingstoke: Palgrave Macmillan, pp. 98–115.

Pachauri, S. (2010) 'The energy poverty dimension of energy security', in B. K. Sovacool (ed.) *The Routledge Handbook of Energy Security*, London: Routledge, pp. 191–205.

Pahle, M. (2010) 'Germany's dash for coal: exploring drivers and factors', *Energy Policy*, 38: 3431–42.

Palacios, L. (2008) 'Latin America as energy supplier', in R. Roett and G. Paz (eds) *China's Expansion into the Western Hemisphere: Implications for Latin America and the United States*, Washington, DC: Brookings Institution Press, pp. 170–92.

Parra, F. (2010) *Oil Politics: A Modern History of Petroleum*, London: I. B. Tauris.

Patt, A. (2015) *Transforming Energy: Solving Climate Change with Technology Policy*, Cambridge: Cambridge University Press.

Pehrson, C. J. (2006) *String of Pearls: Seeing the Challenge of China's Rising Power across the Littoral*, Carlisle, PA: Strategic Studies Institute.

Podobnik, B. (2006) *Global Energy Shifts: Fostering Sustainability in a Turbulent Age*, Philadelphia, PA: Temple University Press.

Pomeranz, K. (2000) *The Great Divergence: China, Europe and the Making of the Modern World Economy*, Princeton, NJ: Princeton University Press.

Prebisch, R. (1950) *The Economic Development of Latin America and its Principal Problems*, Lake Success, NY: United Nations.

Prebisch, R. (1963) *Towards a Dynamic Development Policy for Latin America*, New York: United Nations.

Prins, G. (1990) 'Politics and the environment', *International Affairs*, 66(4): 711–30.

Prins, G. and S. Rayner (2007) 'Time to ditch Kyoto', *Nature*, 449: 973–5.

Rai, A., M. Jain and N. Tomar (2014) 'Last 50 years of hydro energy – a bibliographic survey', *International Transaction of Electrical and Computer Engineers System*, 2(1): 7–13.

Ramamurti, R. (2001) 'The obsolescing "bargaining model"? MNC-host developing country relations revisited', *Journal of International Business Studies*, 32(1): 23–39.

Rangel, L. E. and F. Leveque (2015) 'Revisiting the cost escalation curse of nuclear power: new lessons from the French experience', *Economics of Energy and Environment*, 4(2).

Ratliff, W. (2009) 'In search of a balanced relationship: China, Latin America, and the United States', *Asian Politics and Policy*, 1(1): 1–30.

REN21 (2016) *Renewables 2016: Global Status Report*, Paris: United Nations Environment Program. Available at: http://www.ren21.net/wp-content/uploads/2016/06/GSR_2016_Full_Report.pdf

Renner, M. (2015) 'Post-tsunami Aceh: successful peacemaking, uncertain peacebuilding', in H. Young and L. Goldman (eds) *Livelihoods, Natural Resources and Post-Conflict Peacebuilding*, London: Earthscan.

Rhodes, R. and D. Beller (2000) 'The need for nuclear power', *Foreign Affairs*, 79(1): 30–6.

Rose, T. and T. Sweeting (2016) 'How safe is nuclear power? A statistical study suggests less than expected', *Bulletin of the Atomic Scientists*, 72(2): 112–15.

Ross, M. L. (2012) *The Oil Curse: How Petroleum Wealth Shapes the Development of Nations*, Princeton, NJ: Princeton University Press.

Rosser, A. (2006) 'The political economy of the resource curse', Institute for Development Studies Working Paper 268. Available at: http://www.ids.ac.uk/files/WP268.pdf

Rostow, W. (1960) *The Stages of Economic Growth: A Non-Communist Manifesto*, Cambridge: Cambridge University Press.

Roy, O. (1994) *The Failure of Political Islam*, Cambridge, MA: Harvard University Press.

Roy, O. (2004) *Globalised Islam: the Search for a New Ummah*, London: Hurst.

Rutland, P. (2008) 'Russia as an energy superpower', *New Political Economy*, 13(2): 203–10.

Saad-Filho, A. and J. Weeks (2013) 'Curses, diseases and other resource confusions', *Third World Quarterly*, 34(1): 1–21.

Sachs, J. D. and A. M. Warner (1995) 'Natural resource abundance and economic growth', National Bureau of Economic Research Working Paper 5398. Available at: http://www.nber.org/papers/w5398.pdf

Sachs, J. D. and A. M. Warner (2001) 'Natural resources and economic development: the curse of natural resources', *European Economic Review*, 45: 827–38.

Sakwa, R. (2008) *The Quality of Freedom: Khodorkhovsky, Putin and the Yukos Affair*, Oxford: Oxford University Press.

Sandler, T. and H. Shimizu (2014) 'NATO burden-sharing 1999–2010: an alliance altered', *Foreign Policy Analysis*, 10: 43–60.

Schmidt-Felzmann, A. (2011) 'EU member states' energy relations with Russia: conflicting approaches to securing natural gas supplies', *Geopolitics*, 16(3): 574–99.

Schneider, M. (2013) 'Nuclear power and the French energy transition: it's the economics, stupid', *Bulletin of the Atomic Scientists*, 69(2): 66–76.

Schneider-Mayerson, M. (2015) *Peak Oil: Apocalyptic Environmentalism and Libertarian Political Culture*, Chicago, IL: Chicago University Press.

Schreurs, M. A. (2012) 'The politics of phase-out', *Bulletin of the Atomic Scientists*, 68(6): 30–41.

Schwartz, R. (2008) 'The political economy of state-formation in the Arab Middle East: rentier states, economic reform and democratization', *Review of International Political Economy*, 15(4): 599–661.

Seymour, I. (1980) *OPEC: Instrument of Change*, London: Macmillan.

Shamsul, A. B. (1997) 'The economic dimension of Malay nationalism: the socio-historical roots of the New Economic Policy and its contemporary implications', *The Developing Economies*, 35(3): 240–61.

Shue, H. (1995) 'Ethics, the environment and the changing international order', *International Affairs*, 71(3): 453–61.

Shue, H. (1999) 'Global environment and international inequality', *International Affairs*, 75(3): 531–45.

Shum, R. Y. (2015) 'Where constructivism meets resource constraints: the politics of oil, renewables and a US energy transition', *Environmental Politics*, 24(3): 382–400.

Sieferle, R. P. (2001) *The Subterranean Forest: Energy Systems and the Industrial Revolution*, Cambridge: White Horse Press.

Silver, B. (2005) *Forces of Labor: Workers' Movements and Globalization Since 1870*, Cambridge: Cambridge University Press.

Singer, H. W. (1950) 'The distribution of trade between investing and borrowing countries', *American Economic Review*, 40(2): 473–85.

Slade, R. and A. Bauen (2015) 'Bioenergy resources', in P. Ekins, M. Bradshaw and J. Watson (eds), *Global Energy: Issues,*

Potentials and Policy Implications, Oxford: Oxford University Press, pp. 331–53.

Smil, V. (1994) *Energy in World History*, Boulder, CO: Westview.

Smil, V. (2010) *Energy Transitions*, Santa Barbara, CA: Praeger.

Smith, B. (2004) 'Oil wealth and regime survival in the developing world, 1960–1999', *American Journal of Political Science*, 48(2): 232–46.

Smith Stegen, K. (2011) 'Deconstructing the "energy weapon": Russia's threat to Europe as a case study', *Energy Policy*, 39: 6505–13.

Soares de Oliveira, R. (2007) *Oil and Politics in the Gulf of Guinea*, London: Hurst.

Sovacool, B. K. (ed.) (2011) *The Routledge Handbook of Energy Security*, London: Routledge.

Sovacool, B. K. (2012) 'The political economy of energy poverty: a review of key challenges', *Energy for Sustainable Development*, 16(3): 272–82.

Sovacool, B. K. (2016) 'Differing cultures of energy security: an international comparison of public perceptions', *Renewable and Sustainable Energy Reviews*, 55: 811–22.

Sovacool, B. K. and S. C. Valentine (2010) 'The socio-political economy of nuclear energy in China and India', *Energy*, 35(9): 3803–13.

Srinivasan, T. S. and G. Rethinaraj (2013) 'Fukushima and thereafter: reassessment of risk of nuclear power', *Energy Policy*, 52: 726–36.

Steffen, N., P. J. Crutzen and J. R. McNeill (2007) 'The anthropocene: are humans now overwhelming the great forces of nature?', *AMBIO: A Journal of Human Development*, 36(8): 614–21.

Stern, J. (2010) 'Continental European long-term gas contracts: is a transition away from oil product-linked pricing inevitable and imminent?', *Oil, Gas and Energy Law Intelligence*, 9(1). Available at: https://www.ogel.org/article.asp?key=3075

Stern, N. (2006) *The Economics of Climate Change: The Stern Review*, Cambridge: Cambridge University Press.

Stevens, P. (2006) ' "Resource curse" and how to avoid it', *The Journal of Energy and Development*, 31(1): 1–20.

Stevens, P. (2008) 'National oil companies and international oil companies in the Middle East: under the shadow of government and the resource nationalism cycle', *Journal of World Energy Law and Business*, 1(1): 5–30.

Stevens, P. (2009) *Transit Troubles: Pipelines as a Source of Conflict*, London: Chatham House.

Stevens, P. (2010) *The 'Shale Gas Revolution': Hype and Reality*, London: Chatham House.

Stevens, P. (2013) 'The history of the international oil industry', in R. Dannreuther and W. Ostrowski (eds) *Global Resources: Conflict and Cooperation*, Basingstoke: Palgrave Macmillan, pp. 13–32.

Stevens, P., G. Lahn and J. Kooroshy (2015) *The Resource Curse Revisited*, London: Royal Institute of International Affairs.

Stirling, A. (2010) 'The diversification dimension of energy security', in B. K. Sovacool (ed.) *The Routledge Handbook of Energy Security*, London: Routledge, pp. 146–75.

Stokes, D. and S. Raphael (2010) *Global Energy Security and American Hegemony*, Baltimore, MD: Johns Hopkins University Press.

Stubbs, R. (1994) 'The political economy of the Asia-Pacific region', in R. Stubbs and G. Underhill (eds) *Political Economy and the Changing Global Order*, London: Macmillan.

Stubbs, R. (1999) 'War and economic development: export-oriented industrialization in East and Southeast Asia', *Comparative Politics*, 31: 337–55.

Suny, R. G. (1972) 'A journeyman for the revolution; Stalin and the labour movement in Baku, June 1907–May 1908', *Soviet Studies*, 23(3): 373–94.

Sustainable Development Commission (SDC) (2006) *The Role of Nuclear Power in a Low Carbon Economy*, London: SDC.

Tanter, R. (2013) 'After Fukushima: a survey of corruption in the global nuclear power industry', *Asian Perspective*, 37(4): 475–500.

Thompson, W. (2005) 'Putting Yukos in perspective', *Post-Soviet Affairs*, 21(2): 159–81.

Toke, D. (2013) 'Climate change and the nuclear securitization of UK energy policy', *Environmental Politics*, 22(4): 553–70.

Trainer, F. E. (2007) *Renewable Energy Cannot Sustain a Consumer Society*, Dordrecht: Springer.

Tripp, C. (2002–3) 'After Saddam', *Survival*, 44(4): 22–36.

Tripp, C. (2007) *The History of Iraq*, Cambridge: Cambridge University Press.

Tsie, B. (1996) 'The political context of Botswana's development performance', *Journal of South African Studies*, 22(4): 599–616.

Tyfield, D. (2014) ' "King coal is dead! Long live the king": the paradoxes of coal's resurgence in the emergence of global low-carbon societies', *Energy and Society*, 31(5): 59–81.

United Nations (2010) *Human Development Report 2010*, New York: UNDP.

Unruh, G. C. (2000) 'Understanding carbon lock-in', *Energy Policy*, 28(12): 817–30.

Van de Graaf, T. (2012) 'Obsolete or resurgent: the International Energy Agency in a changing global landscape', *Energy Policy*, 48: 233–41.

Van de Graaf, T. (2013) 'The "oil weapon" reversed? Sanctions against Iran and US–EU structural power', *Middle East Policy*, 20(3): 145–63.

Van de Graaf, T., B. K. Sovacool, A. Ghosh, F. Kern and M. T. Klare (2016) *The Palgrave Handbook of the International Political Economy of Energy*, Basingstoke: Palgrave Macmillan.

Van Groenendaal, W. (1999) *The Economic Appraisal of Natural Gas Projects*, Oxford: Oxford University Press.

Vandewalle, D. (2006) *A History of Modern Libya*, Cambridge: Cambridge University Press.

Velders, G. J. M., S. O. Anderson, J. S. Daniel, D. W. Fahey and M. McFarland (2007) 'The importance of the Montreal Protocol in protecting climate', *Proceedings of the National Academy of Sciences*, 104(12): 4814–19.

Victor, D. G. (2011) *Global Warming Gridlock*, Cambridge: Cambridge University Press.

Vivoda, V. (2009) 'Resource nationalism, bargaining and international oil companies: challenges and change in the millennium', *New Political Economy*, 14(4): 517–34.

Vogler, J. (2016) *Climate Change in World Politics*, Basingstoke: Palgrave Macmillan.

Wallace, W. and A. England (2013) 'South Africa: a faded rainbow', *Financial Times*, 17 February. Available at: http://www.ft.com/cms/s/0/0e7d385e-743f-11e2-a27c-00144feabdc0.html#axzz4IoFoRRZV

Watkins, M. H. (1963) 'A staple theory of economic growth', *Canadian Journal of Development Studies*, 29: 141–58.

Watson, J. and C. Jones (2015) 'Carbon capture and storage', in P. Ekins, M. Bradshaw and J. Watson (eds) *Global Energy: Issues, Potentials and Policy Implications*, Oxford: Oxford University Press, pp. 229–43.

Watts, M. (2004) 'Resource curse? Governmentality, oil and power in the Niger Delta, Nigeria', *Geopolitics*, 9(1): 50–80.

Wenar, L. (2016) *Blood Oil: Tyrants, Violence, and the Rules That Run the World*, Oxford: Oxford University Press.

Wheatley, S., B. Sovacool and D. Somette (2016) 'Reassessing the safety of nuclear power', *Energy Research and Social Science*, 15: 96–100.

Wohlforth, W. C. (1999) 'The stability of a unipolar world', *International Security*, 24(1): 5–41.

World Commission on Dams (WCD) (2000) *Dams and Development: A New Framework – the Report of the World Commission on Dams*, London: Earthscan.

Wright, G. (1990) 'The origins of American industrial success, 1879–1940', *American Economic Review*, 80(4): 651–68.

Wright, G. and J. Czelusta (2004) 'The myth of the resource curse', *Challenge*, 47(2): 6–38.

Wrigley, E. A. (2010) *Energy and the English Industrial Revolution*, Cambridge: Cambridge University Press.

Yates, D. (1996) *The Rentier State in Africa: Oil Rent Dependency and Neocolonialism in the Republic of Gabon*, Trenton, NJ: Africa World Press.

Yergin, D. (1991) *The Prize: The Epic Quest for Oil, Money and Power*, New York: Simon and Schuster.

Yergin, D. (2006) 'Ensuring energy security', *Foreign Affairs*, 85(2): 69–82.

Yergin, D. (2011) *The Quest: Energy, Security, and the Remaking of the Modern World*, London: Allen Lane.

Young, O. R. (2010) *Institutional Dynamics; Emergent Patterns in International Environmental Governance*, Cambridge, MA: MIT Press.

Youngs, R. (2009) *Energy Security: Europe's New Foreign Policy Challenge*, London: Routledge.

Yudin, Y. (2013) 'Nuclear energy and non-proliferation', in A. Goldthau (ed.) *The Handbook of Global Energy Policy*, Chichester: Wiley, pp. 205–23.

Zakaria, F. (2008) *The Post-American World*, New York: W. W. Norton.

Zalaziewicz, J., M. Williams, A. Haywood and M. Ellis (2011) 'The anthropocene: a new epoch of geological time?', *Philosophical Transactions of the Royal Society A: Mathematical, Physical and Engineering*, 369(1938): 835–41.

Ziegler, C. E. (2008) 'Competing for markets and influence: Asian national oil companies in Eurasia', *Asian Perspective*, 32(1): 129–63.

Zubaida, S. (2012) 'The "Arab Spring" in the historical perspectives of Middle East politics', *Economy and Society*, 41(4): 568–79.

Index